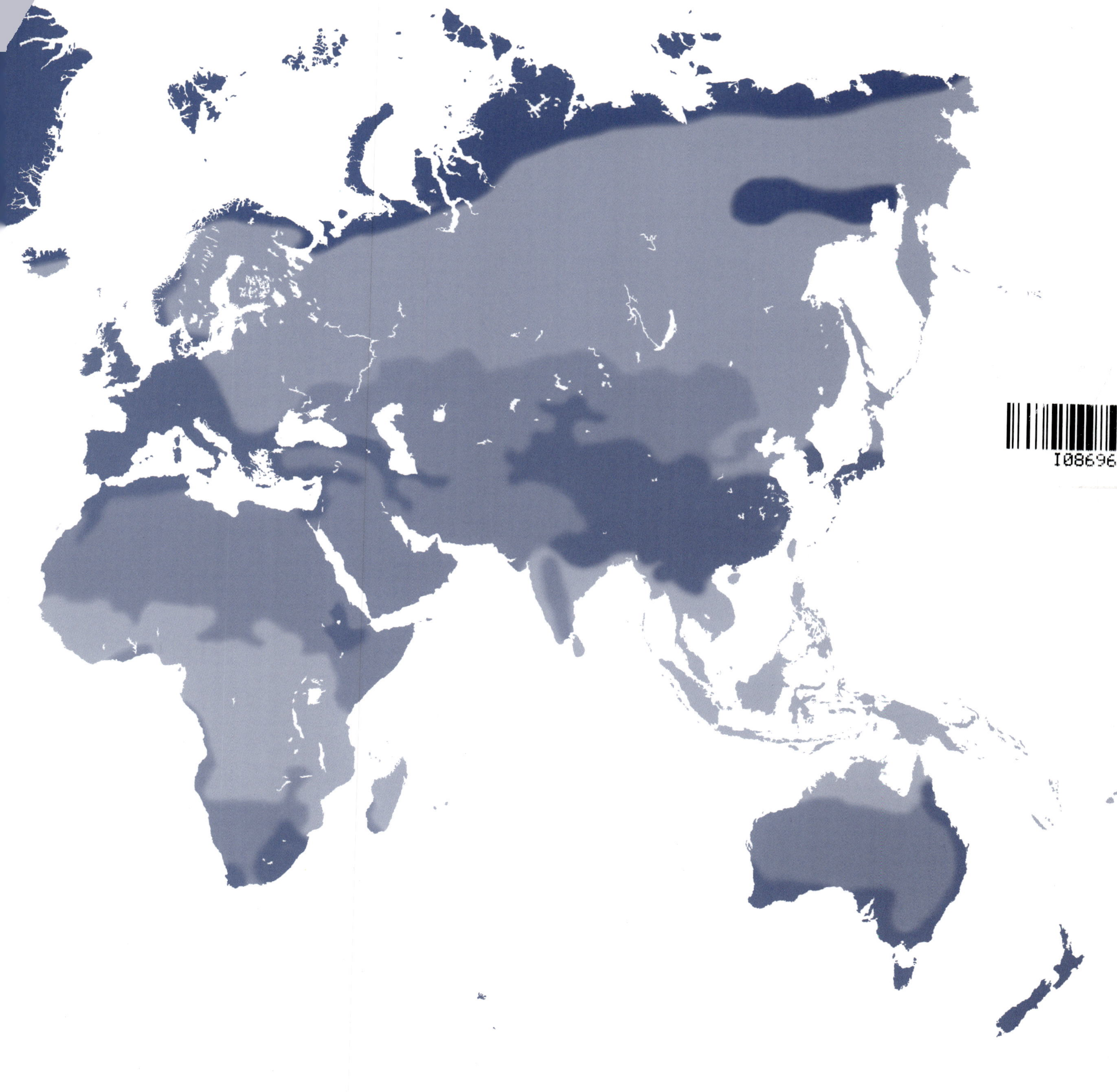

Houses for all Regions

CRAN Residential Collection

AIA
THE AMERICAN INSTITUTE OF ARCHITECTS
CUSTOM RESIDENTIAL ARCHITECTS NETWORK

Houses for all Regions

CRAN Residential Collection

images
Publishing

Published in Australia in 2014 by
The Images Publishing Group Pty Ltd
ABN 89 059 734 431
6 Bastow Place, Mulgrave, Victoria 3170, Australia
Tel: +61 3 9561 5544 Fax: +61 3 9561 4860
books@imagespublishing.com
www.imagespublishing.com

The Images Publishing Group Reference Number: 1054

National Library of Australia Cataloguing-in-Publication entry:

Title	Houses for all regions : CRAN residential collection / American Institute of Architects (AIA).
Author	American Institute of Architects (AIA).
ISBN	9781864705171 (US, UK & Europe, hbk.) 9781864705980 (Asia, Australia, New Zealand, hbk.)
Subjects	Architect-designed houses—United States. Architecture, domestic—United States.
Dewey number	728.370973

Edited by Driss Fatih and Sabita Naheswaran

Designed by Ryan Marshall, The Graphic Image Studio Pty Ltd, Mulgrave, Australia
www.tgis.com.au

Pre-publishing services by Mission Productions Limited, Hong Kong

Printed on 150gsm G-print smooth by Everbest Printing Co. Ltd., in Hong Kong/China

IMAGES has included on its website a page for special notices in relation to this and our other publications. Please visit www.imagespublishing.com.

The editorial team have selected the projects that feature on the jacket.

Contents

Foreword

By Avi Friedman

Throughout most of human history, societies have built dwellings that consider local climatic conditions. The immediate environment was the place from which dwellers also harvested their basic needs. They drew water from streams, grew food, used timber to keep warm and to build shelters. Builders of settlements and homes intuitively integrated vernacular strategies when planning and constructing. Wind direction, sun path and orientation were part of a thought process rooted in knowledge passed on from one generation to the next. Those measures affected the design of the house and the comfort level of the occupants.

The industrial revolution changed all that. When people abandoned farms in search of employment, cities swelled and building methods were altered as a consequence. Construction of dwellings became the responsibility of large organizations that made efficiency the core of their activity. Traditional principles had to be abandoned in favor of those which sped production. Vernacular considerations were victims of this transition. A system and an organization had to be put into place to meet the daily requirements of all the inhabitants—be it food, sanitation or energy. Gradually, homes were linked to utilities like power, fresh water supply and drainage. Perhaps the greatest manifestation of this dependency was the post-WWII suburb. Built away from the city center, a typical sub-division and its single-family detached dwellings consumed valuable resources during construction and after occupancy. Homes were built without regard to orientation, the elements and the site's natural conditions. In addition, chosen planning and construction practices had very little to do with vernacular paradigms. A community was dependent on external sources for its existence and function.

Houses need to go beyond style and respond to vernacular and sociological influences. Celebrating the breadth of quality single family residential work serves as a form of advocacy for the design value of residential architects to the public. Natural and social phenomena have forced us to rethink how development should take place. We began reflecting on issues that were once considered marginal—making them of global concern. They have prompted a search for alternatives to the way we currently house ourselves and force us to revisit past strategies.

Responding to climate and place is possible. I believe that we can indeed design dwellings that reduce dependency on external systems and resources and adopt commonsense, traditional building practices. It would be utopian, but we can design and construct new dwellings where dependence on generic approaches can be substantially reduced.

The outstanding dwellings featured in this book demonstrate that architects and builders can successfully consider and respond to local climatic conditions and natural aspects in their design. Also, that vernacular building practices including use of local materials are becoming part of a vocabulary which is bound to change the way our built environment will look and function in years to come.

Introduction

What makes a good house? The answer to that question is as unique as an individual personality. At the most basic level, a house is a shelter. An individual's basic need is met in relationship to the climate and the resources available. Elegant examples exist of indigenous shelters from all parts of the world. In these shelters, a clear response to the surrounding climate is a primary determinate of form. After the fundamental need of safety and shelter is met, our dwellings become influenced and shaped by culture and community. The design, building, and craft traditions of construction are passed down over time and eventuate in regional style. Finally, at the most intimate scale, houses are inhabited by individuals who outfit their domicile in both functional and decorative ways to express the preferences of the people who call them home.

Vitruvius, a Roman architect, author and engineer from the 17th century wrote in his book *De architectura* that a structure must exhibit the three qualities of *firmitas, utilitas, venustas*. To architects, this translates to "firmness, commodity and delight" and these three guiding principles are still valid when accessing design. Firmness implies a logical, smart structure and high-quality materials. Commodity suggests an appropriateness of function to need and cost. Delight comes from the artful three-dimensional compositions that inspire the soul, and bring joy to each day.

The pursuit of making a good house continues to intrigue and engage us all; perhaps because we know that our houses are the base from which we build our lives. A house itself is the sum of its parts, and the work of architects is the thoughtful assembly of these parts and pieces. Good design balances climate, context and history with current building technology and homeowner values.

This collection of houses is grouped by climatic zones: arid/semi-arid, temperate, tropical/sub-tropical, and arctic/cold-climate. In our increasingly populated world, sensitivity to resources and energy is at the forefront in determining the design of homes. The houses in each zone were designed to respond to climate, while the local culture, materials and craft labor combine to result in different solutions.

Our resources and time are limited, but the possibilities are endless. As you engage in creating a house, let the particulars of your place, your history, and your personality thoughtfully inform the walls that wrap around you, the windows that let the sunshine in and the roof that shelters your thoughts and dreams so that what we collectively build is sustaining and sustainable.

Arctic/Cold-Climate

These regions are characterized by persistent cold and dry weather and relatively narrow annual temperature ranges. Winters include the possibility of 24-hour darkness, with stable, cold conditions and clear skies. Summers are characterized by either long or continuous daylight, occasional damp and foggy weather, as well as rain or snow. Architecture needs to take into account heavy snow loads and harsh prolonged winds.

Tea2 Architects

Lakeside Shingle Style

Minnetonka, Minnesota

The most striking feature of this project is the way it was designed with the main living spaces connected to the outdoors on two opposing sides: a large lake on the southern side and a quaint creek channel on the northern. Having lived on the property prior to demolition of a house that was not designed to take advantage of the unique lot, the owners used to set up lawn chairs on a garage to overlook the serene creek channel on warm evenings. To respond to this desire for double-sided views when the house was rebuilt, the main floor living suite became essentially one space deep, in order to look both ways.

To keep the scale of the house down, the second floor bedrooms and studies were built into the roof space, yielding a story-and-a-half expression. Covered porches and terraces on both aspects provide a gradation of indoor-to-outdoor experiences. Shingle style is suited for the curves and sweeps in plan and roof form and has a precedent on the lake, as several similar lakeside houses attest.

The living room and dining room face the lake but also borrow light and views through the kitchen. The kitchen in turn borrows light and views through the large windows that wrap around the living and dining rooms. The location of the main-level guest suite manifested itself as a curving east wall that terminates in a room dubbed the "Guest Lantern." By sweeping back the guest suite off to the side, this maximizes the creek view from the kitchen and is a welcoming gesture to draw guests to the front door.

A sheltered porch off the kitchen captures the early morning light and offers an escape from the hot midday sun in summer. The south porch provides a sheltered seating area and steps down to a bluestone terrace open to the sky and the shade of an oak tree. This is the casual outdoor dining and entertaining area and has become the owner's favorite space.

To avoid the garage door featuring at the house entrance, and to present a more inviting entry vista, the three-car garage is tucked beneath the guest suite wing and cars enter from the side, preventing the garage mass from blocking views to the creek.

The mechanical system uses geothermal energy as the primary source for heating and cooling. A permeable paver system responds to flood plain and occasional high water conditions. Spray foam insulation is used throughout for an environment where the seasonal temperature difference is 100°F or more (40°C). The cedar shingle roof and walls, along with copper flashing and breathable drainage planes, ensure a long lasting exterior. Clad wood windows have UV-resistant insulated glass that cuts solar heat gain down dramatically from standard insulated glass. A bluestone base and chimney, chosen for durability as well as beauty, root the building to the earth and reduce overall scale.

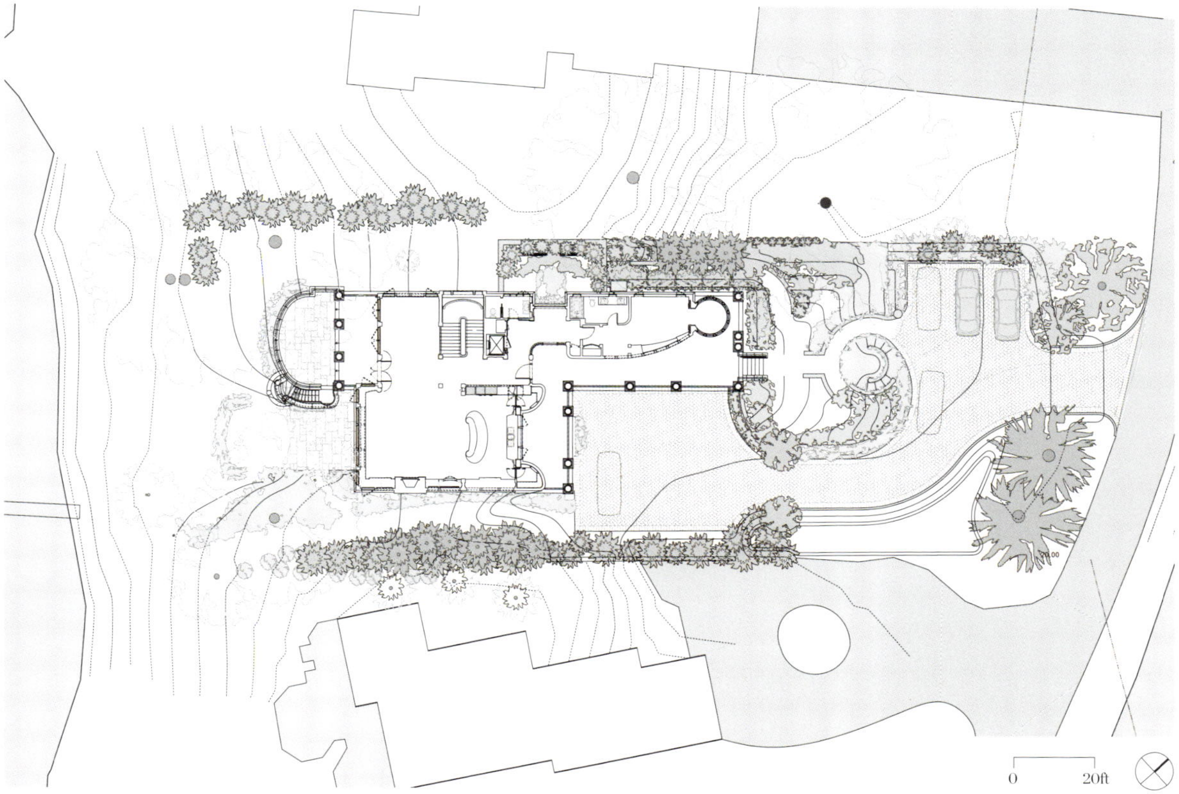

Site plan

DeForest Architects

North Lake Wenatchee

Lake Wenatchee, Chelan County, Washington

Rustic. Modern. Cozy. Sophisticated. This mountain retreat was designed to bridge two worlds with natural ease. Tucked into a sloping site on the north shore of the lake, the house reveals itself as a series of "stops along a trail" that continues through the house to the water's edge. The house is distilled into two simple bars, each with a shed roof. The upper bar contains bedrooms and bathrooms; the lower one is a glassy pavilion that includes the kitchen, living, dining, and screened porch. Every room captures a new and striking view of the lake and the surrounding Cascades. It is a modern design at home in its mountain surroundings. As a four-season retreat, the house is designed to be comfortable for two, yet expand to accommodate a crowd with built-in sleeping nooks, sleeping porch, and a large bunk and TV room hidden behind a hinged bookshelf. Local, durable materials were chosen throughout to reduce maintenance and harmonize with the site.

Lake Wenatchee is located on the east slope of the Cascades below Stevens Pass at an elevation of about 580 meters (1,900 feet). The cold climate is transitional between the alpine climate of the Pacific Crest and the semi-arid steppe of the Columbia Plateau. Temperatures and humidity are similar to the Columbia Plateau; however, Lake Wenatchee is close enough to the crest of the Cascades to average over 4.1 meters (160 inches) of snowfall a season. The site is on the north shore of Lake Wenatchee, with excellent southern exposure and sweeping views of the lake and mountains. The house was sited behind the shoreline trees, allowing the trees to provide summer shade, screen the house from the lake, and frame views of the Cascades. The shed roof on each bar is oriented to shed snow away from the south-facing windows and the access path from the north. The windows remain unobstructed by the winter snows, allowing the low winter sun to shine into the house below the canopies of the screening trees.

The house is engineered to carry substantial snow loads via glulam beams and posts. Radiant heat keeps the house comfortable in the winter while summer sun is controlled primarily through natural ventilation, large overhangs, and careful siting. Cedar, fiber cement, and metal siding are used to reduce maintenance, with particular attention paid to where snow is likely to pile up.

The interior palette builds on the colors and textures of the local landscape. The natural warmth of native Douglas fir and Western red cedar complements the clean lines and simplicity of the North Lake Wenatchee House.

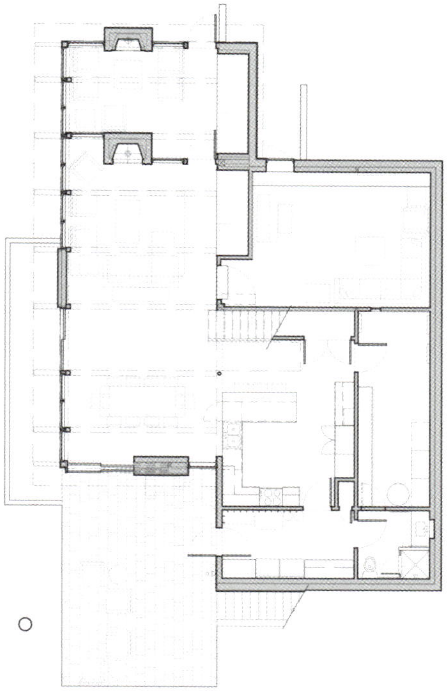

First floor

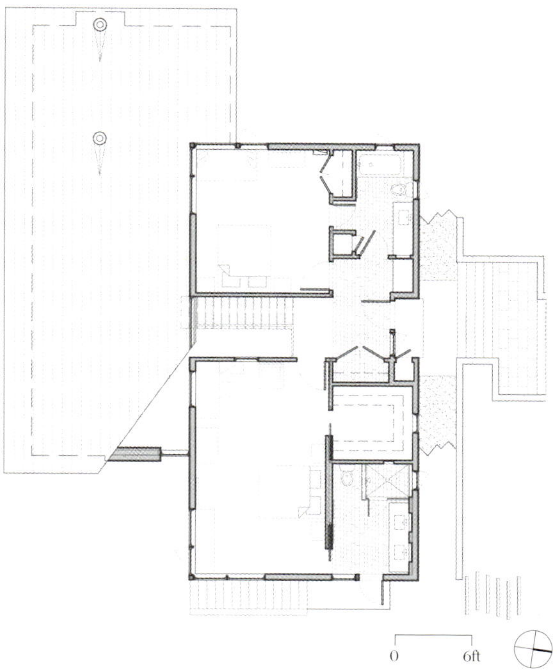

Second floor

Charles Cunniffe Architects

Wrights Road

Aspen, Pitkin County, Colorado

The steep mountainside lot provided the challenges of grade, excessive water, a narrow view corridor, and abundant old growth trees. The homeowner challenged the team to open the views, incorporate the heavy mountainside water, and utilize passive solar energy and ventilation to design a home that could withstand harsh winters and hot summers.

Aesthetically, the owner wished for an open-flowing main level, with a warm yet contemporary color palette. The interior design was to be clean and inviting, and not to be overdone. During the course of design, the owner started a family, thus changing the emphasis of the design from a gentleman's retreat to a family home. The architects worked to accommodate the change while maintaining the sophisticated feel.

To maximize the building envelope, typically architects would position the house against the mountain with views only on one side. The architects instead shifted the house away from the mountain, excavated the hillside and enhanced the waterfall that is enjoyed year round. The home was then designed to sit among the trees, providing 360-degree views and natural light. Staggered rooflines were utilized to capture the views. Grounded in nature, the materials work harmoniously with the site. Exterior materials of Nevada Quartzite, Cambora hardwood, and concrete panels form the exterior and are taken to the interior, to blur the lines between indoors and outdoors.

Large overhangs with hemlock fir soffits provide shelter and shade to the home, while the material palette works to anchor the home to its rugged site. Floor-to-ceiling windows and lift and slide doors open the house completely to the exterior, as operable clerestory windows allow natural light and secure ventilation from mountain critters—a unique situation in the Rocky Mountains.

The best in insulation and Grabill windows and doors create a building envelope that provides a strong barrier to the climatic elements. The home's Savant smart home system allows the owner to control windows, shades, climate, and security remotely.

A large glass pivot entry door opens to a custom walnut and steel, floating staircase spanning three floors. The great room's stone and concrete fireplace is center stage as the juxtaposed kitchen with an oversized "3 Chroma" island and adjacent butlers pantry and bar, opens to the outdoor terrace.

Tucked behind hidden walnut-paneled doors, the master suite opens to an entry gallery, granite fireplace, generous dressing room, and private terrace. The glass shower cube centers the master bathroom with the floating tub looking out to the views. The guest master bedroom is secluded above the garage, while three guest suites, and the home's game/music room are below with a walkout courtyard. The home office/studio space perches above the entry as a tower with 360-degree views and private patio. Photovoltaic panels and the Savant smart home system merge sustainable design attributes with advanced technologies for a state-of-the-art smart home.

Site plan

1 Entry
2 Powder
3 Stair
4 Dining
5 Pantry
6 Kitchen
7 Great room
8 Master bathroom
9 Master dressing
10 Master bedroom
11 Mud room
12 Garage

Temperate

The temperate climate may be defined by what it is not. Not as hot as the tropical/subtropical climate and warmer and milder than the artic/cold. All four seasons are present and obvious. This climate zone requires architecture that can mediate the outside cold and the snow (which is not always present in winter), as well as the summer heat and humidity.

Bohlin Cywinski Jackson

Addition and Restoration of a Historic Cape

Rhode Island

The owners fell in love with coastal Rhode Island and this 28-hectare (70 acres) oceanfront farm two decades ago, and purchased the property after renting it for a succession of summers. The farm, which is comprised of working fields and meadows defined by ubiquitous stone walls and light dappled forest, quietly embodies a modest agrarian character. The farm is surrounded by water on three sides: freshwater ponds lie to the east and west, and the Atlantic Ocean forms the southern border. The cape and a cluster of 18th and 19th-century utilitarian structures occupy a crest at the heart of the property.

The architects have enjoyed a long-term collaboration with the family, whose vision of creating a compound for future generations has been realized through multi-phased renovation, restoration, and new construction that melds seamlessly with the existing structures and landscape. Working closely with the landscape architect and preservation architect, the addition and restoration of a historic cape represents the third phase of cooperative interventions at the farm that reveal the rich variety and nuances of its New England vernacular architecture. The restoration architect was Lombard John Pozzi.

The cape was stripped of its jumbled additions and plumbing and returned to its pure gabled form and function of sitting rooms, sleeping chambers, and hearth room. The addition serves two functions—it houses a kitchen and bath, which allows the cape to serve as a guesthouse, and it provides a kitchen for events held in the nearby barn.

Seen from the exterior, the massing of the addition is smaller, but honors the detail and simple geometric proportion of the historic cape. The interior of the addition is a study in contrasts with its partner. While the cape has low-ceilinged rooms, the interior volume of the addition reveals its tall gabled form in which a freestanding, cherry-clad volume, as meticulously detailed as a piece of fine furniture, contains the bathroom, storage, and kitchen components. Where wood trim in the cape is painted with saturated historic hues, the trim in the addition is painted crisp white.

A 5-meter long (16 feet) glazed passage connects old and new construction. Large expanses of glass were introduced at the addition to distinguish it from the cape's familiar palette of weathered cedar shingles and multi-pane wood windows. The transparency of the addition and link frames views of the original cape and the extraordinary landscape—hay fields, lichen-encrusted silo, fresh water and brackish ponds, and the Atlantic Ocean. The cape, its addition and an adjacent stone barn define comfortably proportioned outdoor rooms, blurring the line between inside and outside.

A new, cast-in-place, concrete watering trough has been positioned along an east–west axis that bisects the centerline of the glazed link. The trough marks the intersection with a north–south axis set during an earlier building phase, carefully knitting together both old and new components of this poignant agrarian landscape.

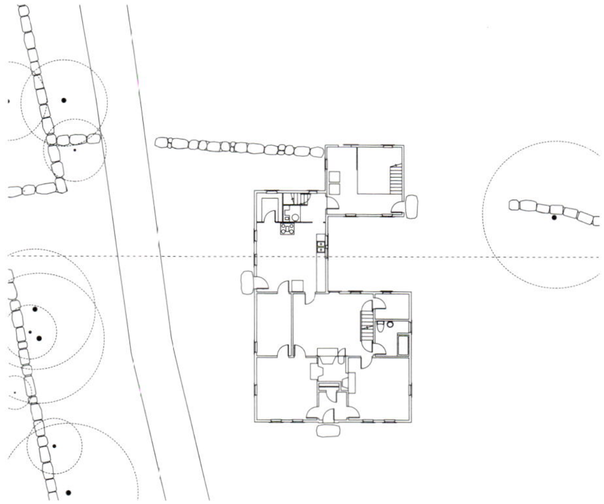

Pre-renovation plan

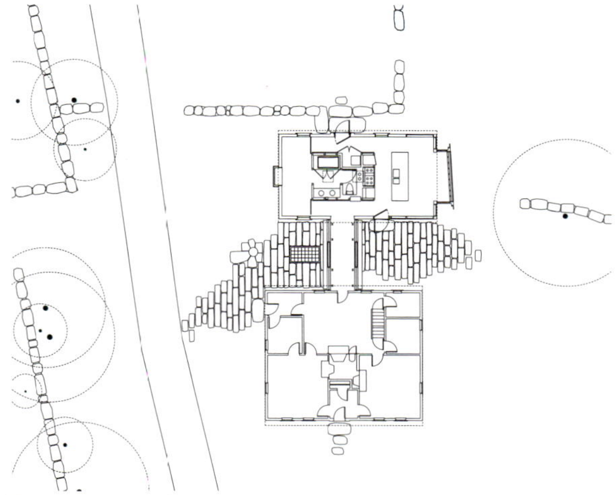

Post-renovation plan

Site plan

Charles R. Stinson Architecture + Design

At Home With Nature

Hastings, Minnesota

The homeowners fell in love with a wooded, secluded lot sloping down towards the St. Croix River Bluffs. They felt at home in the natural setting and built a beautiful pool, yet they felt the existing home was not taking full advantage of the dramatic views and their desire for a more open, light-filled home. For years, they followed the architecture of Charles R. Stinson Architects, including seeing their work at several home tours. Stinson and his team developed a cohesive architectural plan for the site, including a soaring new home perched above the existing pool and a bluff-top art studio on the footprint of the original cabin built on the site. The result is a timeless composition in harmony with the natural surroundings, abundant with light and with a seamless indoor-outdoor flow of space.

This project is a great example of how an architect can help guide a homeowner in being a steward of a natural setting, and how architecture can fully embrace the unique features of a site and create a meaningful connection with nature.

The technologically advanced home features a geothermal mechanical system, a green roof art studio, and triple-glazed high-performance Loewen windows. Extremely durable materials were used inside and out, including clad aluminum, stucco, as well as copper fascia on formal overhangs, which serves to provide shading. Extensive daylighting techniques throughout the home minimize electricity consumption throughout the day, while operable windows promote cross-ventilation. The kitchen also features a highly sustainable and recyclable Valcucine kitchen with natural finishes.

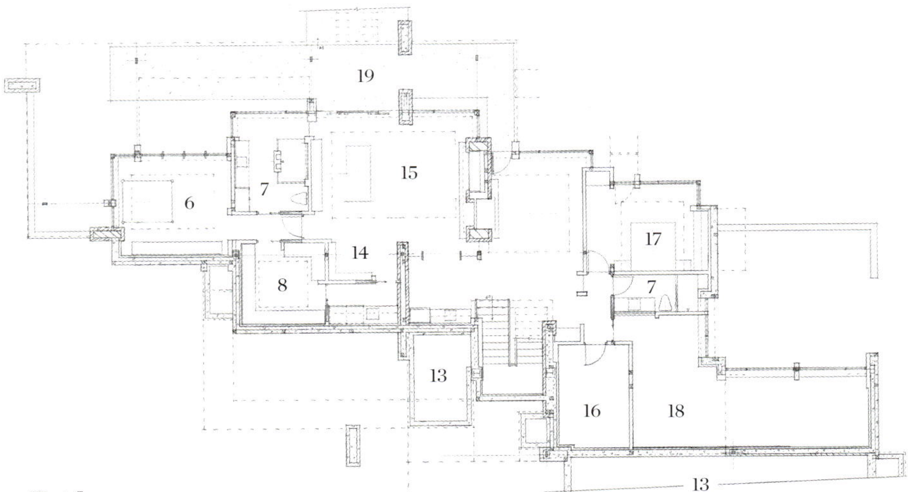

First floor

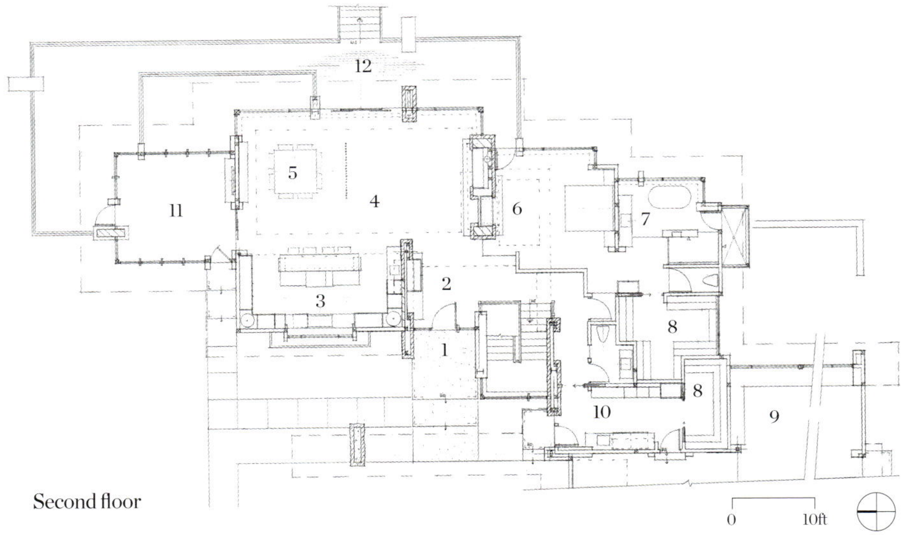

Second floor

1 Entry
2 Entry foyer
3 Kitchen
4 Great room
5 Dining
6 Suite
7 Bath
8 Closet
9 Workshop
10 Laundry
11 Four-season porch
12 Deck
13 Unex
14 Library
15 Office
16 Mechanical storage
17 Guest suite
18 Exercise
19 Terrace

Eck MacNeely Architects

Block Island Residence

Block Island, Rhode Island

A conservation deed restriction limited the size of the house to 230 square meters (2,500 square feet) of living space, but the homeowners wanted to maximize the space, views, and light. That request was made even more difficult because the major views to Block Island Sound were to the north. Turning the long axis of the house east–west maximized the views and burying a portion of the house in a sloping topography gained some essential storage space (not considered living space). Placing a large deck over the lower three bedrooms provided them with views and light and eliminated the curse of a dark space under a deck. Another fourth bedroom was placed just off the entry and a fifth master bedroom was situated off a unique viewing tower on the top floor.

The house was built on one of the last large, elevated pieces of property on Block Island. Every effort was made to maintain the unique quality of the existing landscape, which once contained an orchard, grazing land, meadows, and stone walls. Except for a portion of buried storage space, the topography was changed very little. While the environment can be harsh many months of the year, the summer months can be delightful, and the major rooms of the living space focus on a large deck with folding doors that figuratively and literally connect inside and outside. A folding window was also provided between the kitchen and an exterior island creating a unique kitchen–deck relationship. Traditional forms were used throughout, including a saltbox shape and a tower that echoes a local lighthouse. A small barn reflecting the house shape was also included as a workshop and play space for older children and guests.

Older homes on Block Island are usually quite restrained, reflecting the farming and fishing history of the island. There is also a wide variation in the weather and climate, and house materials have to be appropriate for that condition. Cedar wall shingles and trim along with a metal roof and stainless cables for the rails were deemed consistent with the environment and traditions of the island and somewhat maintenance-free. Clad windows with insulated glass were used along with highly insulated walls and roofs. Large timber trusses and a decorative stair round out the cottage-like quality of the house.

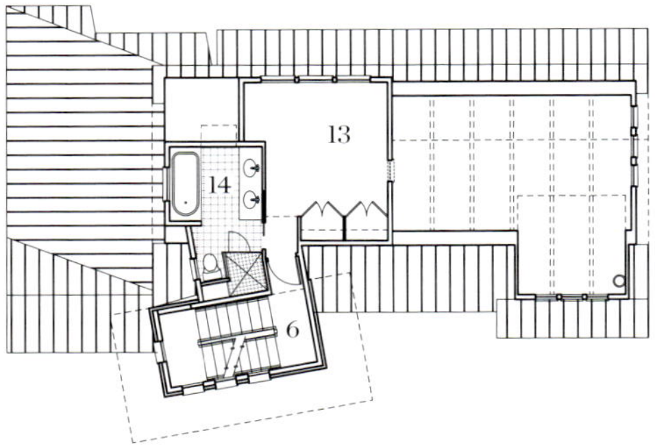

Third floor

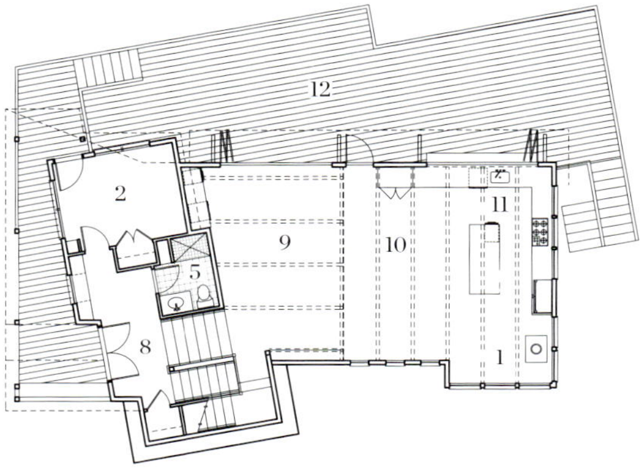

Second floor

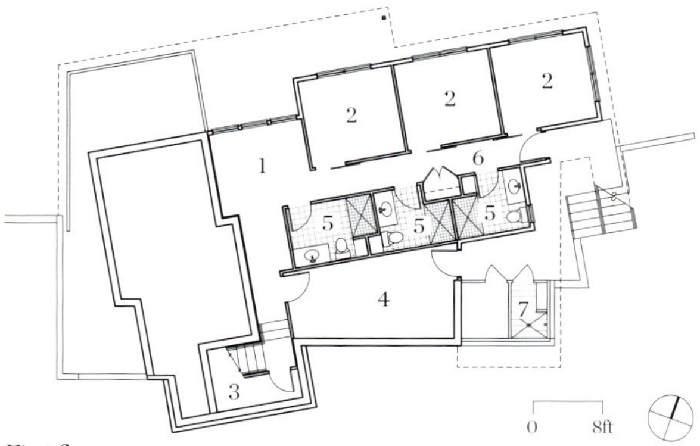

First floor

1 Sitting
2 Bedroom
3 Storage
4 Basement/mechanical
5 Bath
6 Hall
7 Outdoor shower
8 Entry
9 Living
10 Dining
11 Kitchen
12 Deck
13 Master bedroom
14 Master bath

Dettenhausen
18 No.7 93

Joy D. Swallow, FAIA

Buck Hill House

Gerrardstown, West Virginia

Buck Hill House occupies a site located two hours west of Washington, DC, in the Appalachian/Blue Ridge region of West Virginia. The site sits at the prow of a mountain on a 1.6-hectare (4 acres) site in a rural setting. The site is surrounded by steep drops in elevation and is heavily wooded with oak forest. A spectacular 180-degree view of the "continuous" West Virginia mountain ranges lies southwest of the site.

It was designed for an artist and art historian who had lived two separate professional lives for nearly 20 years. The 230-square meter (2,500 square feet) house represented the first home where both were able to merge their diverse and rich collections of books and art. The house was conceived as a retirement retreat, and needed to incorporate universal design standards. The couple had an extensive library and art collection that required special attention. A linear corridor/library with flanking bookcases serves as a repository for their collections and books. Light monitors punctuate the length of the linear corridor, allowing natural light to enter into the center of the house.

The owners desired visual connections to the outside, balanced with vistas created within the house that included framed views of their significant print collection. Cross axis points bisect the central corridor and created a weave of nature and art. The overall form of the house consists of two rectangular blocks that shift from one another and are connected by the linear corridor/library space. The public spaces—living, dining, and kitchen—are oriented toward the southwest views and outdoor terrace. The loft-like space has elements that define each of these spaces within the larger whole.

The ceiling above the dining room area has been suspended from the ceiling, creating an intimate dining area. The ceiling and attached wall are painted graphically, which accentuates and contrasts with the larger vaulted space on both sides. The fireplace acts as a large sculptural element that defines the living and dining room. The master bedroom suite on the southeast is self-contained and private. The couple hosts many guests and they requested separation between the master suite and guest room. The larger bedroom off the living room doubles as an office space and guestroom. For larger public functions, the double doors from this space open to extend the public space.

The use of mass-production techniques, standardized, off-the-shelf parts, simplicity of form, and the integration of indoors and outdoors were central to the development of the project. Using materials that were off the shelf and readily available kept the budget in check. The exterior is faced with 4 x 8 concrete board with exposed off-the-shelf metal channels. The 4 x 8 grid minimized waste and streamlined the building process. The house is painted in colors derived from the geology of the site, as the owner wanted the house to recede into its natural setting and become part of the site. The sloping roof is sheathed in a dark standing seam metal.

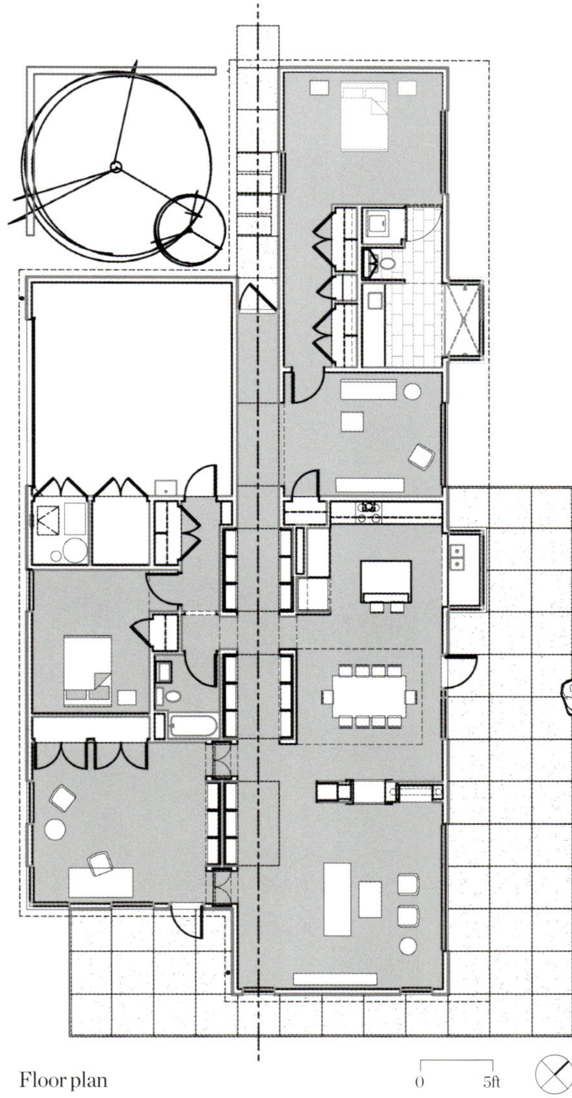

Floor plan

Balance Associates, Architects

Capitol Hill Residence

Seattle, Washington

The Capitol Hill Residence is located on a ridge with sweeping views of the surrounding lakes and mountains. At three stories, and under 265 square meters (2,865 square feet), it is a compact family home. Sustainable systems include rainwater collection, solar panels, mechanical blinds for solar shading, and geothermal wells, in addition to standard sustainable building practices such as high levels of insulation, low-e glazing, daylighting all spaces, and environmentally friendly materials.

The architect collaborated with a team of geothermal, civil, and structural engineers as well as solar designers and landscape architects, to arrive at a building that is both environmentally sustainable and high-tech. There are integrated systems at work to heat the home in winter, cool it in summer, maintain indoor air quality year round, ensure natural light reaches all interior spaces, store rainwater, and harness solar power.

The house's massing is a result of maximizing the spaces that face the eastern view, while minimizing the overall footprint of the building on site. While the eastern façade of the house is primarily glazed, the other three sides are largely opaque, with areas of translucency for privacy from neighbors to the north. In order to get daylight to the center of the house, a sloped translucent roof spans the length of the house and filters daylight. Even on a cloudy Seattle day, the house is very well day-lit.

Green land-use strategies include pavers widely spaced apart to allow planting inbetween; greenscreen, a grid structure that provides space for plants to infill it; and promotion of an onsite ecosystem on the eastern slope. Landscape design incorporates features to infiltrate storm water on site, to minimize water usage and reduce maintenance. The planted area comprises northwest natives that thrive in the wet winter/dry summer environment.

Some of the sustainable systems are architectural in nature. For example, the roof rainwater collects into a steel entry water feature, daylight from a typical overcast Seattle sky penetrates deep into the house through a central translucent slot, and exterior mounted mechanical shades prevent excessive heat gain without sacrificing the view. Hidden systems affect energy consumption, such as the buried geothermal wells and heat pumps that aid in heating and cooling, and a 30-panel photovoltaic system that feeds electricity back to the grid.

Acrylic cantilevered treads with glazed guards and railings keep the stair light and airy, allowing living and dining spaces to flow together. Durability comes largely from the use of long-lasting materials, such as concrete-based stucco on a rainscreen system that rarely needs to be replaced, or resealed; a low-maintenance, long-lasting rain screen with modified wood panels; and a steel structure with ipe wood for the decks. The Capitol Hill Residence is more than 'green,' it is a high-performance house that is both environmentally sustainable and high-tech.

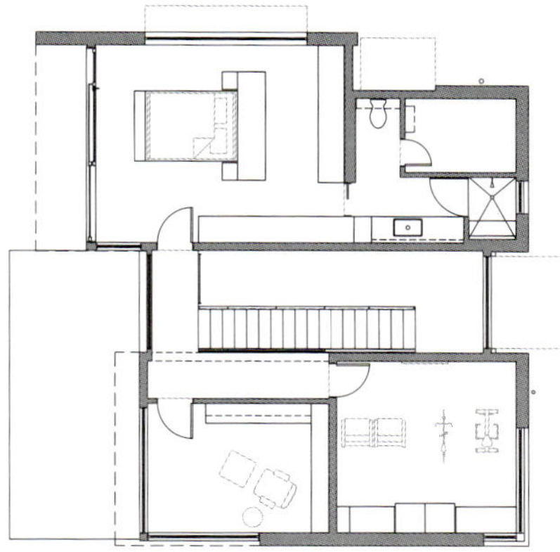

Second floor

First floor

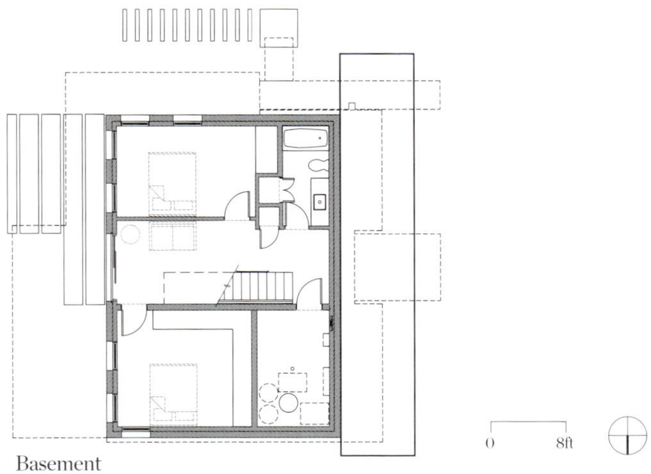

Basement

Stuart Cohen & Julie Hacker Architects LLC

Craftsman House

Suburb of Chicago, Illinois

The house was designed to suit the informal lifestyle of a couple with grown children who entertain civic and charity groups in their home. The clients wanted a contemporary version of an Arts and Crafts house. They loved bungalows and the houses of Greene and Greene, collected South American and African folk art, and wanted a house that could display the things they own. Their large suburban corner lot has views of Lake Michigan across a public park and they wanted outdoor living spaces, a roof terrace facing the lake, and a private rear yard for a swimming pool.

The house is located on a lake front street only five blocks long. These blocks comprise large early 20th-century houses, which are predominantly Georgian and Tudor in style, along with several large Prairie houses designed by the Prairie School architects, Tallmadge and Watson. The new house maintains the scale and visual variety of the street. The house is sited with the main rooms and their continuous rows of French doors facing east to the lake and opening onto a raised terrace sheltered and shaded by a projecting canopy.

The house is a combination of local Wisconsin limestone and cedar shingles with a standing seam metal roof. The roofing material was chosen because the prefinished color of the roofing could be matched to the color of the metal-clad casement windows. The house is insulated with a combination of closed and open cell spray insulation and wet and dry blown cellulose. All mechanical equipment and appliances are high efficiency and the house's mechanical systems are a combination of electric radiant floors, geothermal heating and cooling, and an energy recovery system integrated with the heating and cooling system. Because of the high water table on the property there is a system of underground water retention tanks, which store groundwater for landscape irrigation and to seasonally fill the swimming pool.

The design team was comprised of Stuart Cohen, Julie Hacker, with Garry Shumaker as the project architect; interior furnishings were provided by James Dolenc and Thomas Riker of jamesthomas, LLC; Kettelkamp & Kettelkamp were the landscape architects; and the general contractor was Sturm Builders Inc.

101

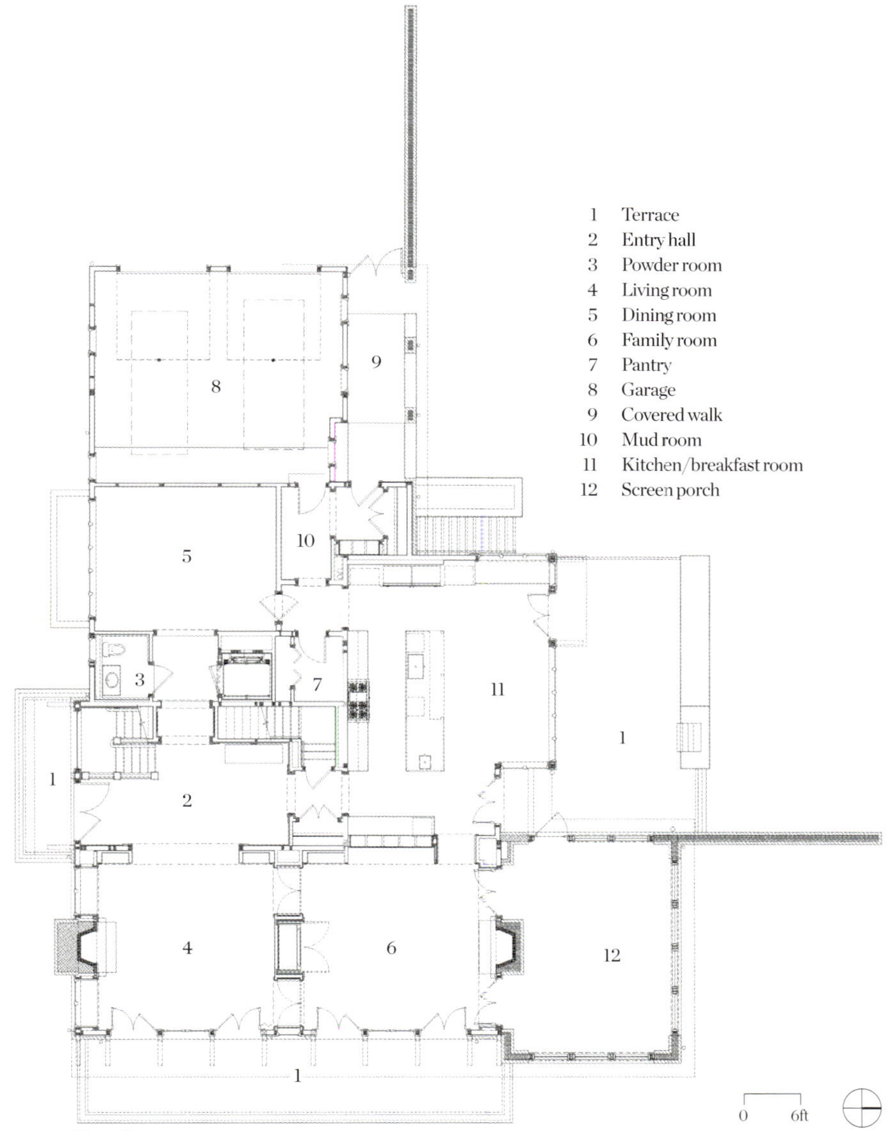

1 Terrace
2 Entry hall
3 Powder room
4 Living room
5 Dining room
6 Family room
7 Pantry
8 Garage
9 Covered walk
10 Mud room
11 Kitchen/breakfast room
12 Screen porch

First floor

nonzero\architecture

Crestwood Hills Residence

Los Angeles, California

The project's massing consists of a simple large glass volume for the shared living spaces, wrapped around three-dimensionally by a solid band of smaller rooms. This concept allows for complete openness to the surrounding nature, yet naturally maintains the family's privacy from the street. By carefully calibrating the views, controlling the sun and the wind, the design responds intimately to the site. Closely integrated into the historic hillside surroundings, the house features a typical transparent clerestory above its opaque walls and is shaded by a floating flat roof with exposed steel beams. Throughout the house, views of the canyon, trees, and the distant ocean are framed for maximum enjoyment, as well as privacy.

Spaces are extended outward and the surrounding landscape is continually incorporated into the design. The entry sequence leads through the solid perimeter band of rooms, through a glazed door sheltered by a continuous skylight, into the large space, which finally opens up dramatically after one passes behind the freestanding kitchen volume. The always present inside–outside relationships, openness, and attention to craft and detailing were achieved with a glazed steel post-and-beam structure. The concrete retaining walls are left exposed where possible and contrast with the steel and the sustainably harvested tropical hardwood siding. Built-in mahogany cabinets and shelves keep the tall main space open and uncluttered. A fully rotating bookshelf separates a study in the solid band of rooms from the living space and offers access as well as a choice between shelves and a normally concealed television. The house is inspired by the strict regulations in the historic neighborhood, which demand a mid-century ideal of a rustic, humane Modernism. Appreciative of these values, the design is a contemporary interpretation and celebration of their inherent qualities, with an even greater focus on sustainability. View preservation and a sensitive approach to the down-slope site dictated the single-story massing from the street. A low profile and the careful positioning of the volumes make the comparably large home appear modestly scaled, in keeping with the neighborhood. Photovoltaic glass panels power the house and offer serene dappled light on the large deck, while they help shade it along with deep roof overhangs. Natural ventilation is facilitated through the placement of operable windows and folding glass walls along the path of the prevailing breezes.

The benign Mediterranean climate of the hills along the Westside of Los Angeles is ideal for an open and airy design and the house takes full advantage of the opportunities afforded by it. The post-and-beam construction blends in with the context of surrounding mid-century houses and provides transparency and maximum integration into the natural hilly environment. Existing trees were retained as much as possible and contribute to the feeling of a mature environment. Roof beams from the old house were repurposed as exterior steps and benches throughout and complement the drought-resistant landscape planting.

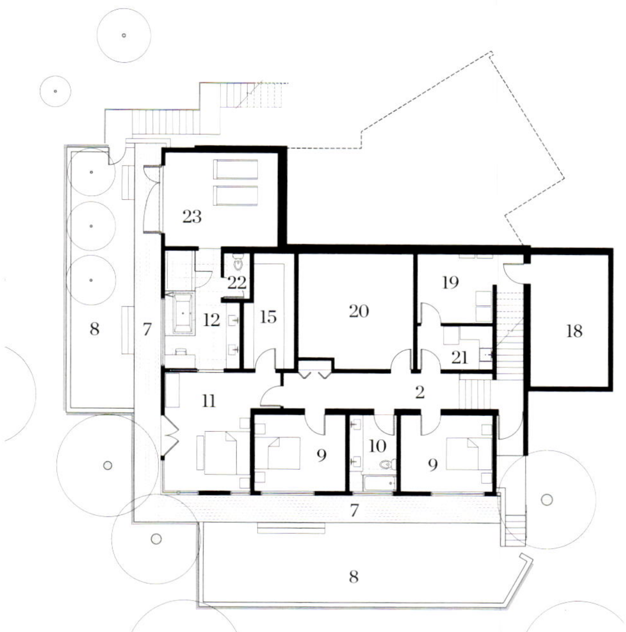

First floor

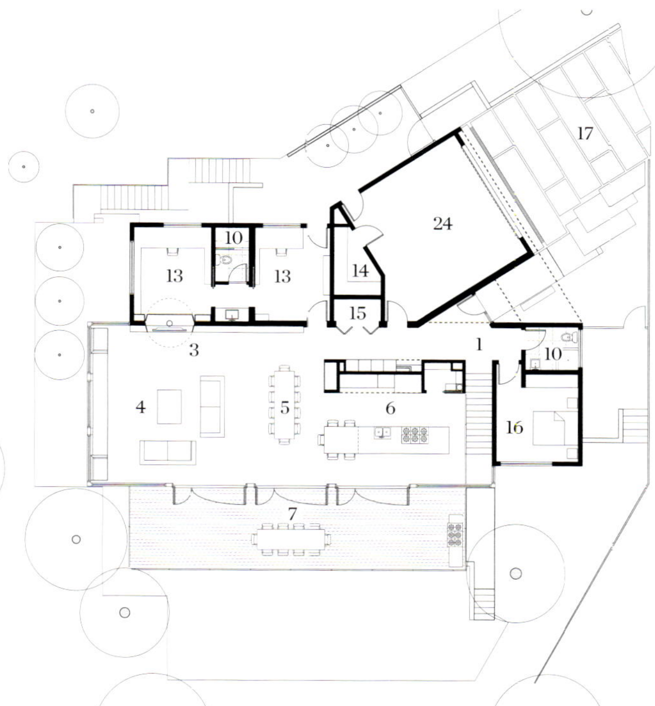

Second floor

1 Foyer
2 Hall
3 Revolving bookshelf
4 Living room
5 Dining room
6 Kitchen
7 Deck
8 Lower yard
9 Bedroom
10 Bathroom
11 Master bedroom
12 Master bathroom
13 Study
14 Storage
15 Closet
16 Guest room
17 Driveway
18 Crawl space
19 Mechanical room
20 Basement/storage
21 Laundry
22 Toilet room
23 Gym/rec. room
24 Garage

0 10ft

Studio/Durham Architects

D&MF Residence

St. Louis, Missouri

The client's brief was to replace a poorly maintained 1920s era house with a new design for their young family and art collection that would take better advantage of the features of the existing site. The design solution located the new structure at the top of the property, close to the building set back line, in the area of the site with the most existing tree cover. This location allows all the main living spaces to open to the views down the wooded rolling hillside to the south, allowing the house to feel as if it has no neighbors.

The new house was configured as a modified 'H' to visually protect the central two-sided glass walled living space, with support spaces placed along the private access lane/driveway side. To the north, against the busy access road, a sunken private courtyard defined by a retaining wall and a landscaped berm protects the living areas visually and from traffic noise. The wing furthest from the private lane includes the master suite with the children's bedrooms on the level above. An existing cow pond was retained as a design feature and used as a storm water retention area.

The house includes multiple high-efficiency mechanical systems divided into five zones for both comfort and to maximize performance, and the shell was sealed tightly and super insulated wherever possible. Windows were laid out in all the wings to provide through breezes in mild weather. A commercial grade store front system was used on the exterior, and the house was clad in Midwestern sourced limestone veneer and a rain screen system of tropical hardwood installed on battens. The clean modern lines of the new house echo the post-war modern design homes that used to dominate the neighborhood, but have since been replaced by McMansions.

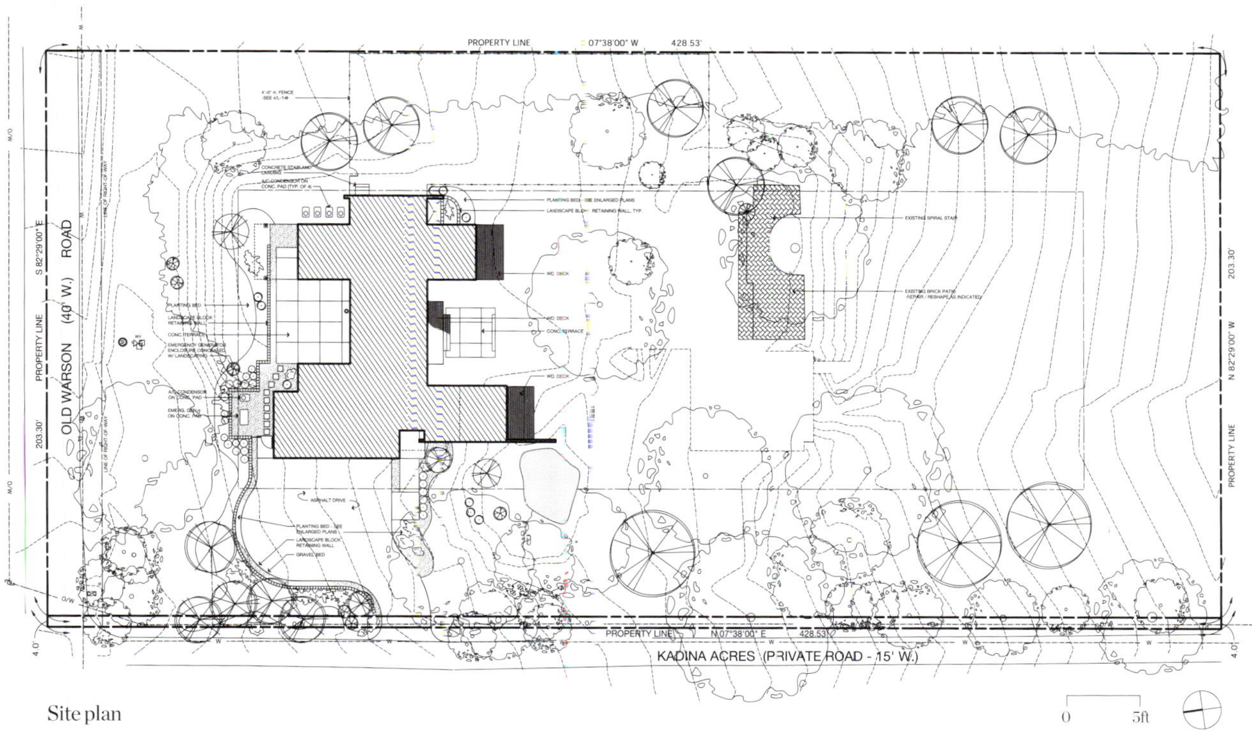
PROPERTY LINE
07°38'00" W
428.53'
OLD WARSON (40' W.) ROAD
PROPERTY LINE
S 82°29'00" E
203.30'
203.30'
N 82°29'00" W
PROPERTY LINE
PROPERTY LINE
N 07°38'00" E
428.53'
KADINA ACRES (PRIVATE ROAD - 15' W.)
0
5ft

Site plan

Terry & Terry Architecture

Diamond Project

San Francisco, California

The Diamond Project is a dwelling that responds to the character of its site and environment while accommodating the needs of a family. The main floor sits at garden level, and contains the common spaces. The kitchen spills through a wall of glass into a backyard patio, which leads through a garden to a small satellite structure, which serves as a home office. Stairs from the living room lead to a roof deck which functions as a continuation of the garden living space. The roof deck also provides a unique connection to the surrounding hills speckled with dwellings of the San Francisco neighborhoods. The lower portion of the dwelling holds the less public spaces—guest room, children's playroom, and utilities. An ample, yet thoughtful selection of glazed openings gently brings daylight into the home, and makes the best of views allowed by the site. Concrete walls form the sides of the house, and continue to the rear to enclose the backyard. This use of concrete provides thermal mass, which buffers the house from temperature swings, which increases energy efficiency.

The structure uses sloping roof planes that hover above the main floor, and are contained between the longitudinal concrete walls, evoking the hills and valleys of the surrounding area. Strategic gaps or fissures were formed between roof and walls to illuminate the walls with natural light. Large glazed openings in the front and rear of the house create transparency between indoor and outdoor spaces that share the language of simple materials and clean detailing throughout the dwelling. This aesthetic creates the warmth and calmness essential for a family in an urban setting, without distracting from the simple beauty of well-juxtaposed spaces.

The sides of the house are formed by concrete walls, which also enclose the backyard. A third concrete wall extends vertically from the garage structure below to form the fireplace and chimney. This use of concrete provides thermal mass for energy efficiency. The concrete absorbs heat energy during the day, keeping the interior comfortable, and helping to maintain a moderate, baseline temperature for the cooler evenings. Since the house is located in a relatively dense urban area, the concrete walls also add protection against fire.

Between the perimeter concrete walls, the architect used a combination of transparent glass and wood-skinned wall. The ipe wood skin is devised as a double wall system, in which horizontal ipe strips are placed over vertical, furring strips. This allows ventilation between the skin and the underlying wall, thus avoiding heat build up in the wall and interior spaces.

The architect used extensive glazing to allow natural light in, capture views, and provide connection to the outdoors. To accomplish this, they used a reinforced concrete column formed from the window seat in the rear to provide lateral support for the structure.

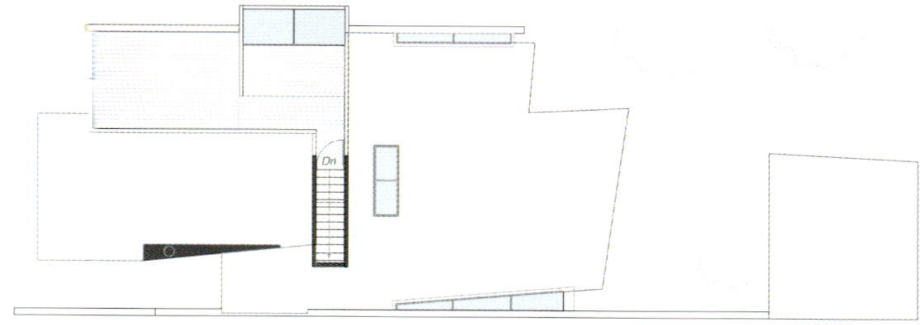

Roof/deck

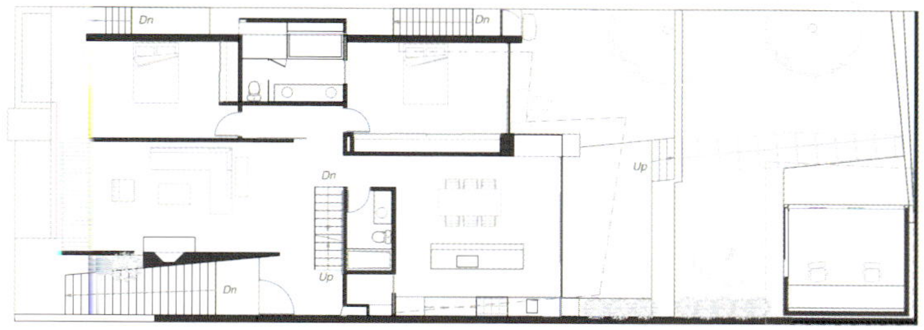

Main floor

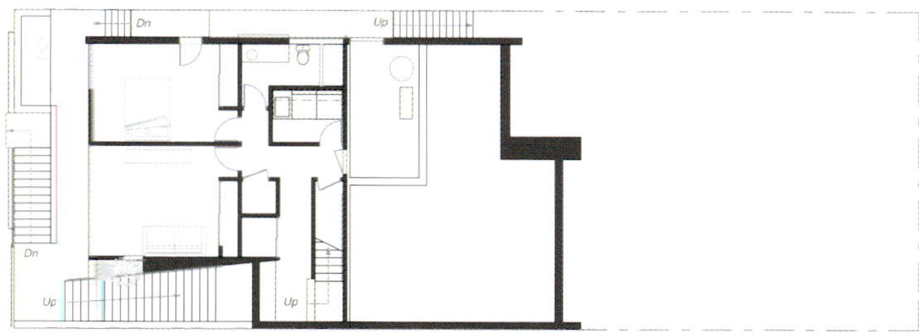

Lower floor

Garage

dSPACE Studio

Historic Wicker Park

Chicago, Illinois

The owners of this 1880s Italianate home wanted to add a contemporary living space. The design direction was to create a modern interpretation of an orangery—a glass structure used as a conservatory, common in England, where the owners had lived. The program called for a great room, patio, and roof deck, with integration of interior and exterior spaces.

The resulting addition is a two-story steel and glass volume attached to the rear of the historic home with an operable 5-meter (17 feet) glass door adapted from the aircraft hangar industry. This bifold door completely integrates the interior to the landscaped yard, and, when open, becomes a canopy to protect the patio from rainfall.

The stained concrete floor in the addition blends with the limestone patio, easing the transition from interior to exterior space. A hanging FireOrb heats the space and can be rotated 180 degrees to face the patio, at times functioning as an outdoor fireplace.

An interior steel and oak staircase and catwalk connect to an exterior spiral staircase, leading to an intimate roof deck with a sunken lounge area protected by native grasses, built-in hot tub, and space for a small vegetable garden.

Green design elements include LED lighting, rainwater collection, drought-tolerant plantings, high-efficiency mechanicals, and infrastructure for future solar panels.

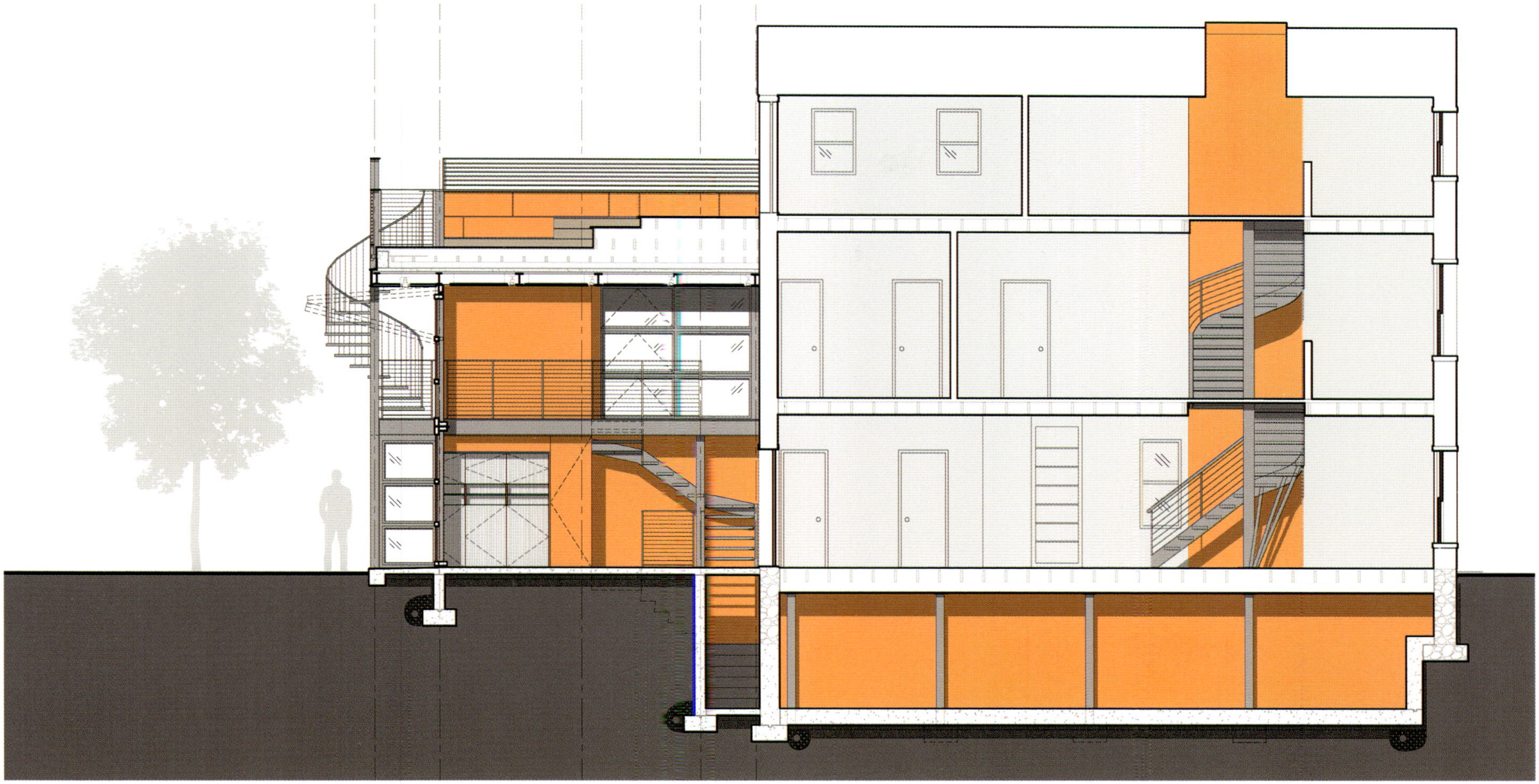

Section

Polhemus Savery DaSilva Architects Builders

House on the Cove

Cape Cod, Massachusetts

The front of the House on the Cove is welcoming, as well as formal and symmetrical. A small courtyard space is enclosed on three sides by the house, and by landscape walls on the fourth. A super-sized fan-light over flat, broad columns marks (and also symbolizes) entry. The gabled bay in which the screen wall sits is smaller than the gable ends that flank the sides of the courtyard. It is balanced, however, by secondary gables that are similar in scale and that set slightly forward of the larger gables. The scale of the screen wall, however, highlights its symbolic role in the overall architecture and landscape. It is scaled more to that overall context than it is to the immediately adjacent courtyard. The actual entry is tucked into the corner of the porch created by the screen wall.

The strength of the image allows an irregular plan to accommodate the internal needs without reducing the formality of the entry court and front façade or the power of the entry symbolism. Where the front is an expanded and formalized "cape," the back, facing an ocean cove and the open ocean in the distance, is more irregular, more massive, and shaped around maximizing water views. The architect feels it is more in the tradition of a grand shingle-style cottage. A re-centering around three lines occurs between front and back. This creates a subtle order that keeps the plan classical on the one hand and casual on the other.

While the historic vernacular form, a low gabled cottage with gridded double hung windows, is much beloved as a symbol of the "simple life," the actual type did not suit the client of this project. They sought a house that was compatible with the vernacular type, prevalent mostly in expanded 1970s to 1990s versions in their neighborhood, but that was also at once grand and formal for entertaining, and relaxed and playful for everyday living. The architect's solution provides a formal expanded cape style at the front, and a picturesque shingle style at the back where the scale of the waterfront context and the desire to have a full two stories capturing views implied a different architecture. Strict conservation requirements for the top-of-coastal-bank site allowed only as much disturbance to the ground as a previously existing house on the property.

Gray shingled houses with white trim are the most common vernacular on Cape Cod. This project continues the tradition. A house of similar size, built within the last 50 years, had existed on the property, but the quality of both the design and construction was sub-standard. The new home has high-efficiency systems, insulated low-e glass, tight house detailing, and an upgraded septic system that all improve environmental responsiveness. It also takes advantage of the special site characteristics, maximizing water view and relationship to mature plantings at the front.

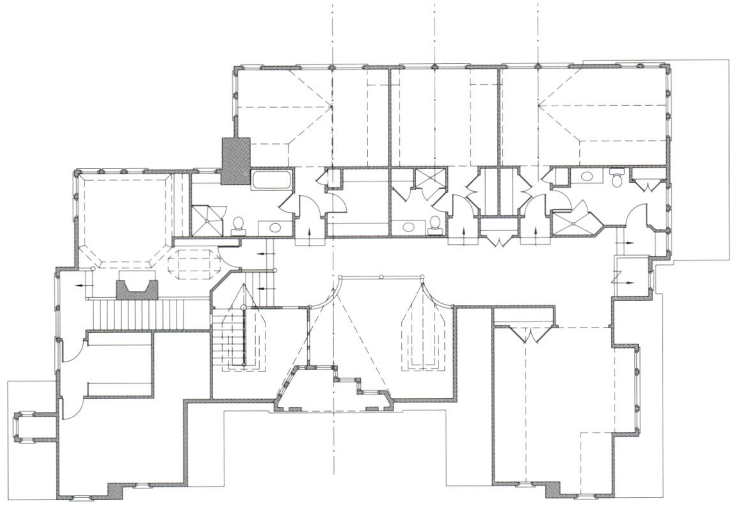

Second floor

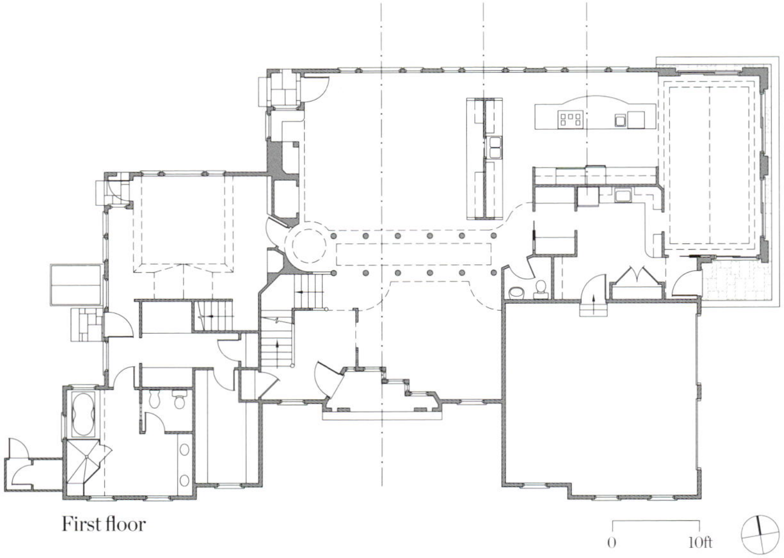

First floor

Uli and Associates

Hudson Valley Country House

Hudson Valley, New York State

The Hudson Valley Country House is a daring double-footprint project that is defined by its public and private spheres, oversized windows, and multiple terraces. The house is a response to an extensive and dynamic program that began with a kit, brought to this rocky, wooded plot in custom-designed prefabricated parts, bolted together and, once finally assembled, clad in an envelope of soft wood panels so that modern and rustic were at one. A mostly open-plan ground floor offers a kitchen, dining and living area, and a grand 9-meter (30 feet) indoor pool with woodland views to create a single merged space as inviting in winter as it is in summer. When designing the home, architect Ulises Liceaga was very interested in the play of lines, inside and out. At the same time, he was deeply inspired by artist Diego Rivera and Frida Kahlo's artist studio back in his hometown of Mexico City—a major cultural landmark built in 1930. The studio, and very much the relationship of the two artists, was both connected, yet still apart. The footbridge consists of a single tilted stanchion and cables that suspend the walkway; it takes its inspiration from the angles, orientation, and axis of the main building to which it leads.

When designing the house, Liceaga had an ecological responsibility in mind. Among the strategies proposed to economize without compromise, he used "reclaimed" materials wherever possible: for example, all the closets were built from retail display furniture bought as scrap from a dismantled Virgin Records store in Manhattan. Salvaged theater light fixtures were refurbished and incorporated into a custom lighting system for the entire house. Continuing in the same fashion, most of the furniture for the house came from refurbished old family heirlooms. Century-old chairs were tactfully refinished and reupholstered to respectfully dialog with the "country-modern" typology of the Hudson Valley dwelling. Most of the home's bright colors are confined to the private areas, whereas the earth tones and subdued metallic hues characterize the public realm. The exterior is cedar cladding with ipe timber on the bridge and all the decks—ipe is one of the hardest and most durable timbers available.

In addition to using reclaimed materials throughout, to further strengthen the environmentally responsive design, the pool was designed to eschew chlorine and other chemical cleansers in favor of the ozone filtration system.

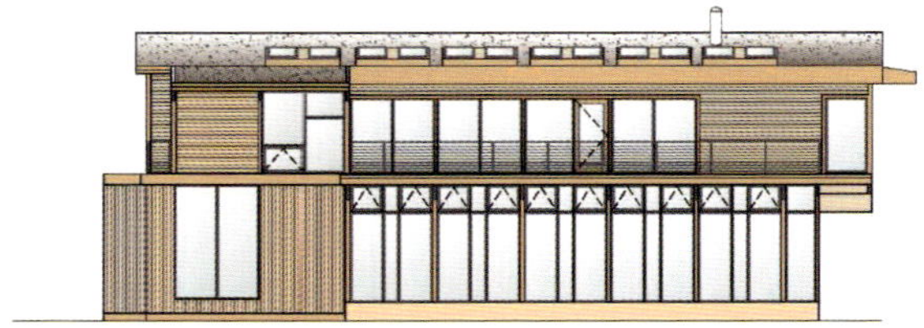

East elevation

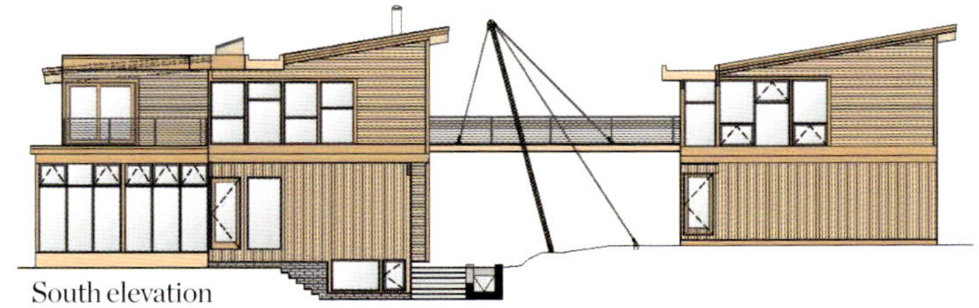

South elevation

West elevation

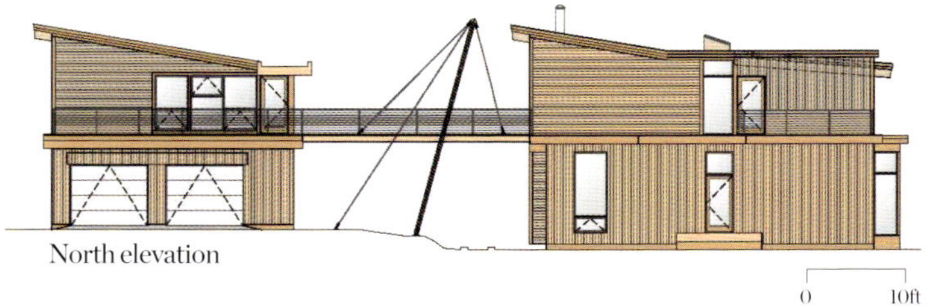

North elevation

WNUK SPURLOCK Architecture

In | Out

Stinson Beach, Marin County, California

This new single-family residence is situated along the mountainous coastline north of San Francisco in Marin County, California. The house is designed to be open to the landscape, yet provide a private sanctuary for its occupants. The main entry is hidden between two volumes, thereby creating a sense of privacy and seclusion from the street below. However, once inside, the building opens up to the outdoors, taking advantage of spectacular views of the surrounding natural environment. Nearly every room contains large floor-to-ceiling windows, providing spectacular views of the ocean and parkland, and the numerous terraces, roof decks, and balconies accentuate a blending of interior and exterior spaces.

The topography, orientation, views, and zoning restrictions strongly influenced the design concept. The lot is a rectangular 2,045 square meters (22,000 square feet) with 40 meters (130 feet) of street frontage. Conceptually the building is a series of one-story volumes that step up the site, following the existing grade. This idea simultaneously addresses the grade change and zoning codes that restrict roof heights to 5 meters (17 feet) above grade, while reducing the scale of the building.

Organized around a central courtyard, the home was configured to address the topography, orientation, and views of the Pacific Ocean and state park and is reminiscent of a small clustered village. The structure is physically divided into two sections by a courtyard: one section will be for the family; the other, a guest wing and pool house. The family section takes advantage of the ocean views and runs along the western side of the site. The guest section runs parallel to the south property line. Besides living, gathering, dining, and cooking spaces, the house contains four bedrooms, five baths, a two-car garage, utility areas, a pool house, pool, sauna, and spa.

Besides the orientation and configuration, the residence is integrated into the site through the use of sustainable materials and technology. Vegetative roofs filled with regional plant material reduce stormwater runoff and help the building blend into the natural environment. Pervious paving at the driveway and numerous outdoor terraces also aid in reducing storm water runoff. The building is energy efficient, using solar systems for both heating and hot water systems. An efficient, single-room width design and placement of large operable windows on opposing sides of the structure take advantage of natural breezes off the ocean, allowing air to pass through the building, providing natural cooling and eliminating the need for mechanical air conditioning systems.

Sustainable products are used throughout the residence: concrete and bamboo flooring, high-efficiency plumbing fixtures are used in the interior, and recyclable metal studs and steel for structure. The exterior is sheathed in a combination of natural and recycled materials. Fiber cement panels in natural hues, and metal panels of copper patina and bronze-coated zinc help identify spatial functions within the residence and blend into the natural environment.

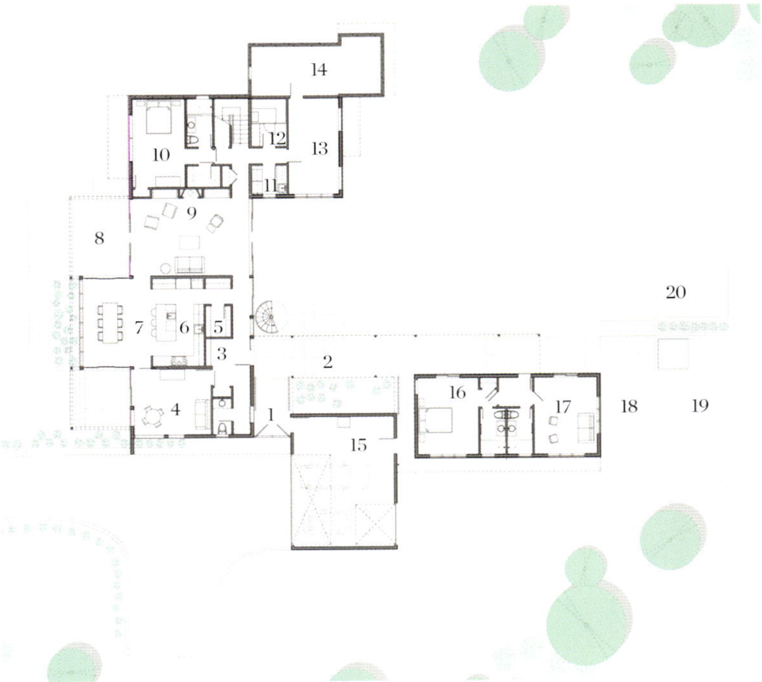

1 Entry
2 Central courtyard
3 Foyer
4 Library
5 Pantry
6 Kitchen
7 Dining room
8 Front patio
9 Living room
10 Bedroom
11 Laundry
12 Sauna
13 Work room
14 Storage
15 Garage
16 Guest suite
17 Bunk room
18 Pool-side patio
19 Pool
20 Terrace patio

0 10ft

Floor plan

HENRY MOORE

Hutker Architects, Inc.

King's Shade

Falmouth, Massachusetts

"King's Shade" sits on the water's edge overlooking the entrance to Falmouth Harbor and to the bay beyond. The 890-square meter (9,600 square feet) gambrel roof house was designed to "fit in" to the historic, turn-of-the-century architecture that dominates the peninsula known as Chapoquoit Island, while at the same time providing the owner with the benefits of modern living on the inside.The house takes advantage of the gentle slope of the grade towards the water by providing four levels of waterview living spaces, including a walk-out lower level.

Unique features included accommodating the client's specific program requirements into a relatively small footprint on a sloping site, all while respecting the historic neighborhood and trying to "fit in." On the outside, the classic gambrel shape echoes the turn-of-the-century shingle style architecture that was prevalent at the time of the island's original development. However, this historic shell encloses cutting-edge technology and numerous modern amenities, many of which are also disguised on the interior. These conveniences include top-of-the-line fixtures, appliances, finishes, and technology systems. A dedicated home theater has also been integrated into a full lower level space below the garage, utilizing a pre-cast concrete slab system to support the weight of the vehicles parked above without the need for structural columns.

The layout of the interior spaces is also "modern" in the sense that consideration was given to how and when the client will occupy the house. The mechanical systems and the spaces that they serve were designed to accommodate year-round and seasonal use, allowing for selective conditioning of some, but not all spaces, when needed. The spaces were also designed to be lifestyle-friendly, providing the flexibility for large gatherings, often focused around the kitchen, family, and dining rooms, while maintaining the intimacy of private spaces for children and adults alike.

The project features standard and pink granite, which comes from West Falmouth and is heavily used in the region thanks to its composition and availability. Alaskan yellow cedar shingles are used for the roof and siding because of their durability and longevity compared with other types of cedar. The existing stone wall was restored and rebuilt in its original location in front of the home. A hydro-air system and densely packed cellulose insulation create an exceptionally efficient structure. Other materials include granite and soapstone countertops; custom stone fireplaces; antique oak, antique chestnut, teak, and holly wood flooring; and reinforced concrete foundations.

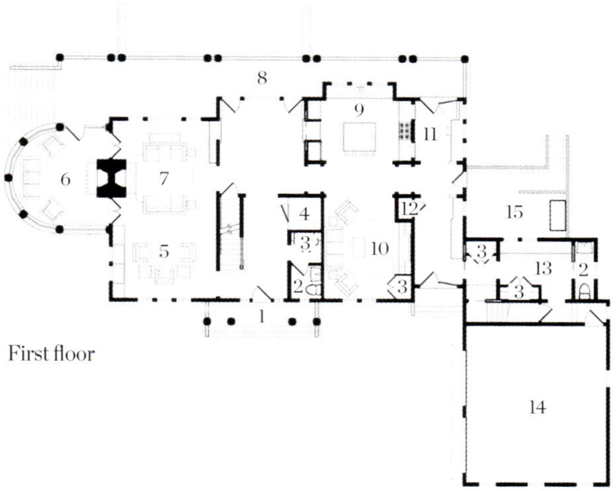

First floor

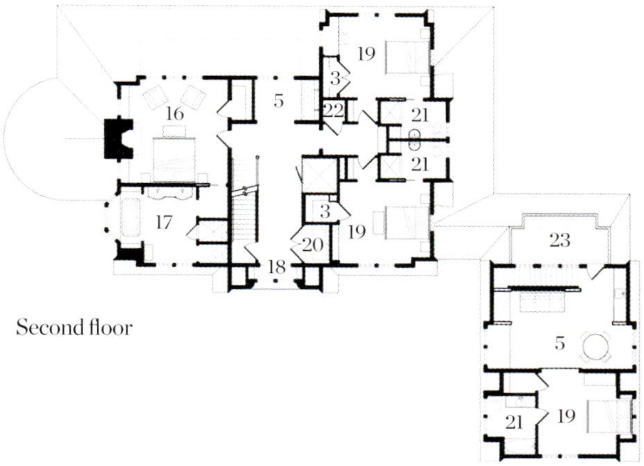

Second floor

1 Entry porch
2 Powder room
3 Closet
4 Elevator
5 Sitting area
6 Screened porch
7 Living room
8 Covered porch
9 Kitchen
10 Family room
11 Family office
12 Pantry
13 Mud room
14 Garage
15 Terrace
16 Master bedroom
17 Master bathroom
18 Reading alcove
19 Bedroom
20 Laundry
21 Bathroom
22 Linen closet
23 Deck

0 10ft

Lake Forest Park, Washington

Located on a secluded, wooded site about 25 miles north of Seattle, a 1950s northwest contemporary house has been completely renovated while retaining the spirit of the original house. With extensive new windows and glazed roof monitors, the renovated house appears as a glass pavilion in the forest.

The floor plan has been re-organized to create a spacious, light-filled master bedroom and master bathroom, with each space surrounded by glass and views to the forest. The main living and dining spaces have been slightly enlarged, and a new roof monitor with high windows has been added to bring in soft natural light. The enlarged kitchen has counters in quartz and cast-glass, with continuous windows extending directly to counter level.

The existing hemlock ceiling with exposed fir beams in roughly half the house has been retained, and new fir ceilings have been added to the remainder. The existing terrazzo flooring has been re-finished, with new areas of terrazzo added in a complementary color.

Consistent with the original simplicity and clarity of the house, a palette of new materials has been added to create powerful juxtapositions of texture and color, allowing each material to benefit from adjacent contrasting surfaces. Casework consists primarily of cherry panels: some panels are smooth, while others have been milled with a CNC (computer numeric controlled) router to make a texture evocative of "woven wood." A 9-meter long (30 feet) accent wall adjacent to the dining and kitchen areas has been clad entirely in weathered steel panels. Suspended casework on the steel wall utilizes either resin panels with natural grasses or textured cherrywood, set against the variegated umber colors of the steel.

In keeping with other FINNE Architects projects, this renovation has pursued the idea of "crafted modernism," the enrichment of a modernist aesthetic with highly personal crafted materials and objects. Custom fabrications included the cast-glass kitchen counter, steel wall panels, mirror frames, shade valences, lighting bars, hand-blown glass light fixtures, and a number of custom furniture pieces. The glass wall between the master bedroom and bathroom has been transformed with the use of a hand-drawn pattern in etched glass, with the pattern being more dense at the bottom (for a sense of privacy) and increasingly transparent at the top.

Sustainable design practices have been integral to the project. Radiant heating under terrazzo flooring has created an even heat source with maximum energy efficiency. High clerestory windows bring natural light deep into the house and motorized operators allow venting during summer months. Many green materials (resin panels, quartz counters, linoleum, low VOC paint, and sustainable wood products) have been used. But above all, it is the fact of renovation itself that is inherently sustainable and captures all the embodied energy of the original 1950s house, which has now been given a fresh life. The renovation also speaks to a very important sustainable principle: build it well and it will last for many years!

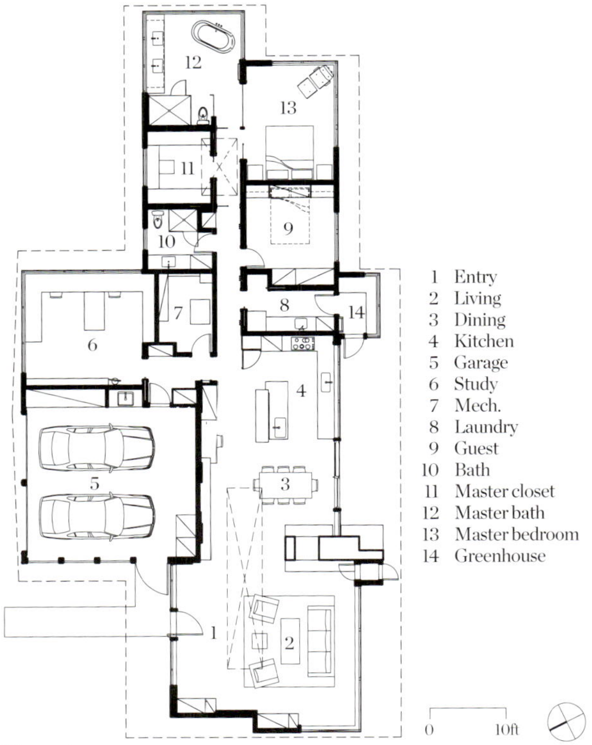

1 Entry
2 Living
3 Dining
4 Kitchen
5 Garage
6 Study
7 Mech.
8 Laundry
9 Guest
10 Bath
11 Master closet
12 Master bath
13 Master bedroom
14 Greenhouse
0
10ft

Floor plan

Gelotte Hommas Architecture

Lakefront Splendor

Mercer Island, King County, Washington

In the 1960s the house was ahead of its time, but time—and lifestyles—had passed it by. The architect's clients wanted to bring the home into the 21st century and transform it into "a house for entertaining—warm with an edge to it, classy but casual."

Adjusting the floor plan allowed for wide open spaces, and room for a stunningly warm, inviting place to gather. Both inside and out, finishes were upgraded, details enriched, and the inside spaces were opened to the refreshed landscaping. The clients are fortunate to live in an environment that draws people outdoors, and this home takes full advantage of that. A palette of wood, steel, and stone gave the home deep warmth, while clearly saying "this is a very modern house!" Every surface was transformed with fine materials and distilled details.

Sun shading trellises made of steel and wood were added above the windows and doors to soften the harsh sun. This detailing informed the design of the outdoor entertaining area, as well as the re-imaged front entry. An existing space between the house and the detached garage was filled with a new office space, while the garage itself was transformed into a showroom for the client's collection of cars. The new kitchen, richly clad in cherry, is designed to handle large parties, as well as every day cooking. Likewise, the master suite is clad in rich stone and stunning woodwork, creating a place where you feel pampered every day.

Through sophisticated detaining and careful choice of materials, this home has definitely been "fast-forwarded" into the modern era with both grace and swagger.

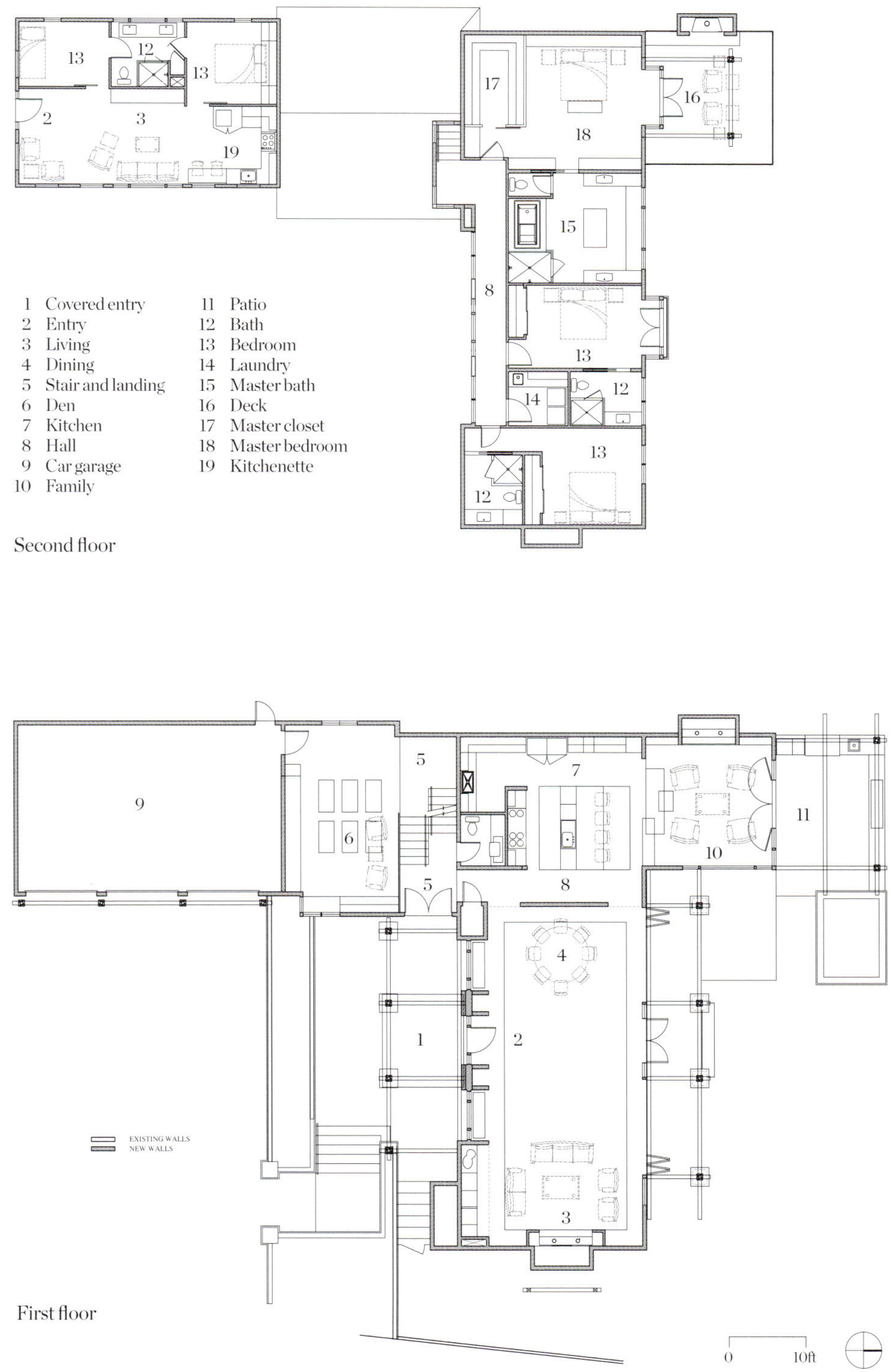

1 Covered entry
2 Entry
3 Living
4 Dining
5 Stair and landing
6 Den
7 Kitchen
8 Hall
9 Car garage
10 Family
11 Patio
12 Bath
13 Bedroom
14 Laundry
15 Master bath
16 Deck
17 Master closet
18 Master bedroom
19 Kitchenette

Second floor

First floor

Estes/Twombly Architects

Maple Hill

Westwood, Massachusetts

From the beginning, the clients wanted a house that would be integral with the landscape. With the architect, they looked at several sites, deciding on a parcel of more than 8 hectares (20 acres) with a long north–south ridge opening to a bowl on the west and the south.

The driveway skirts the west face of the ridge with the house sited perpendicular to the ridge about two-thirds of the way into the site. The long, one-story plan consists of two gabled forms separately containing the bedrooms and the living area, connected by a lower pitched roof containing the entry and study. The low profile nestles into the site, a counterpoint to the tall surrounding pine trees. The ridge slopes down from the bedroom wing, giving privacy to the rooms above, with a playroom below.

The living side of the house sits close on a terraced plinth that starts at the connector and wraps around the south and west sides of the house. A stone wall retains the downhill side of the driveway. The pool and barn are tucked in beside this wall, sheltered from north winds and open to the west and south. Stone landscape walls extend into the house and vice versa, separating the public courtyard from the private terrace areas.

Exterior materials include stone, glass and wood. The New Hampshire granite arrived in 1.8-meter by 1.8-meter by 0.6-meter (6 feet by 6 feet by 2 feet) monoliths and was worked on-site in a manner reminiscent of New England cemetery walls: large rough-faced blocks with narrow chinking. Wide, rough-sawn red cedar boards clad the house, installed horizontally as clapboards with pronounced mitered corners. Windows and doors are custom made.

Inside, dark wood trim and cabinetwork punctuate the light colored walls and furnishings, deliberately kept neutral to avoid competing with the ever-present landscape. The linear plan is simple, with all major rooms opening to the bowl to the south and west. Wide eaves shade these south-facing windows. The final house and landscape work in concert and are a testament to the owner's vision and commitment. The builder was Old Grove Partners of Needham, Massachusetts and the landscape architect was Stephen Stimson Associates of Cambridge.

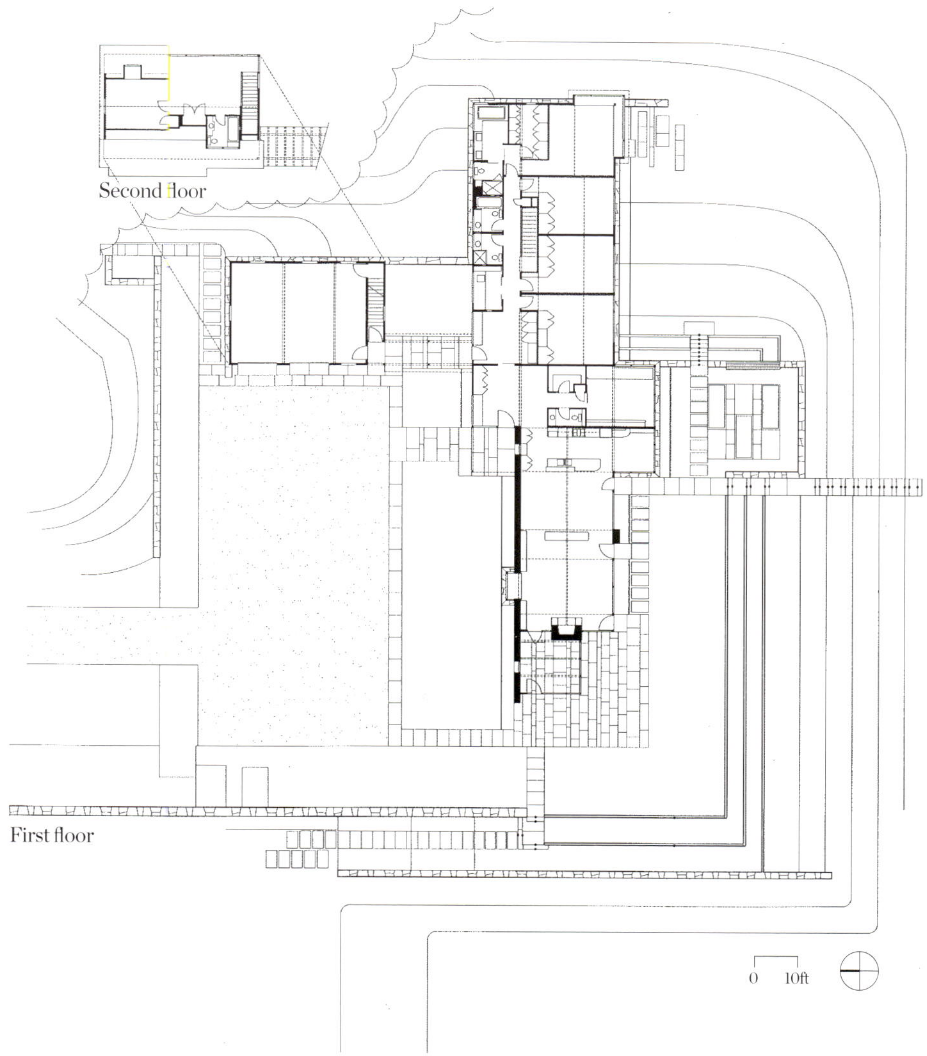
Second floor
First floor
0 10ft

The University of Tennessee College of Architecture and Design / Tricia Stuth, Robert French, and Richard Kelso

The New Norris House

Norris, Tennessee

The New Norris House is a single-family dwelling that is modular, prototypical, and resource efficient. It is located on a previously developed infill lot in Norris, Tennessee, a New Deal town created by the Tennessee Valley Authority. One of the first planned communities in the United States, it is now listed on the National Register of Historic Places. Key components of the community were the Norris Houses, homes built as models of modern, affordable, and efficient living. These homes integrated new technologies of the time—municipal electricity, water, and sanitary systems—and incorporated new materials and building techniques. The New Norris House commemorates the 75th anniversary of the TVA's Norris Project and seizes the opportunity to reconsider the shape of the landscapes, communities, and homes of today.

A LEED for Homes Platinum project and an AIA COTE Top Ten Green project, the New Norris House pursues high performance building through traditional and innovative means. The design uses vernacular form, made contemporary through taut details and bright, airy interiors. At 94 square meters (1,008 square feet), it is less than half the size of the median US house, sited on a 0.1 hectare (0.3 acre) lot.

Stewardship, innovation, and the betterment of society were central to the original Norris project and are the core of contemporary sustainable design. Sustainable principles in this project include the synthesis of performance and aesthetic experience; reciprocity between built and natural environments; a multidisciplinary collaborative design team; and vernacular lessons updated through technical innovation. Natural, durable materials that improve with weathering resonate with the historic context and include locally sourced Atlantic White Cedar, coated steel and salvaged white oak flooring.

The spatial composition and placement of apertures are optimized to create an open, bright, and spacious interior volume; balance connections to the public street and forest preserve; and leverage useful solar gain and natural ventilation. Thoughtful passive response allows for the minimizing of active systems.

Offsite construction and panelized, prefabricated, and modular units led to a 70 per cent diversion of construction waste. Advanced framing techniques resulted in a 17.5 per cent reduction in lumber, increased insulation, and decreased thermal bridging. A ventilated rainscreen façade resists moisture and decay and highly insulated walls reduce heat transfer. Efficient integrated equipment includes a solar hot water system, ductless heat/air systems, energy recovery ventilation, and ceiling fans. Collected roof water is treated for non-potable uses and graywater is managed on-site.

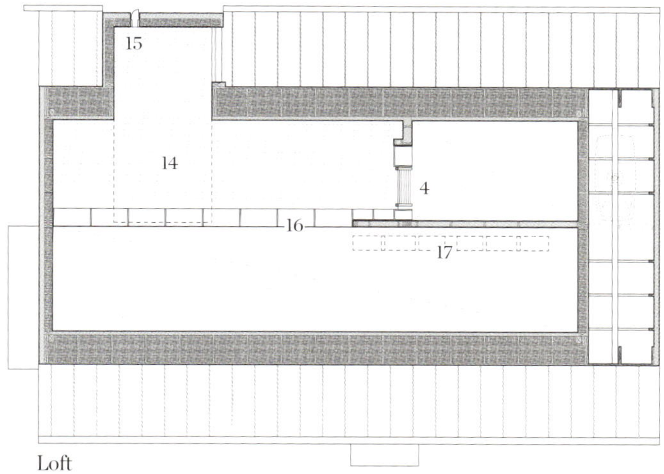

Loft

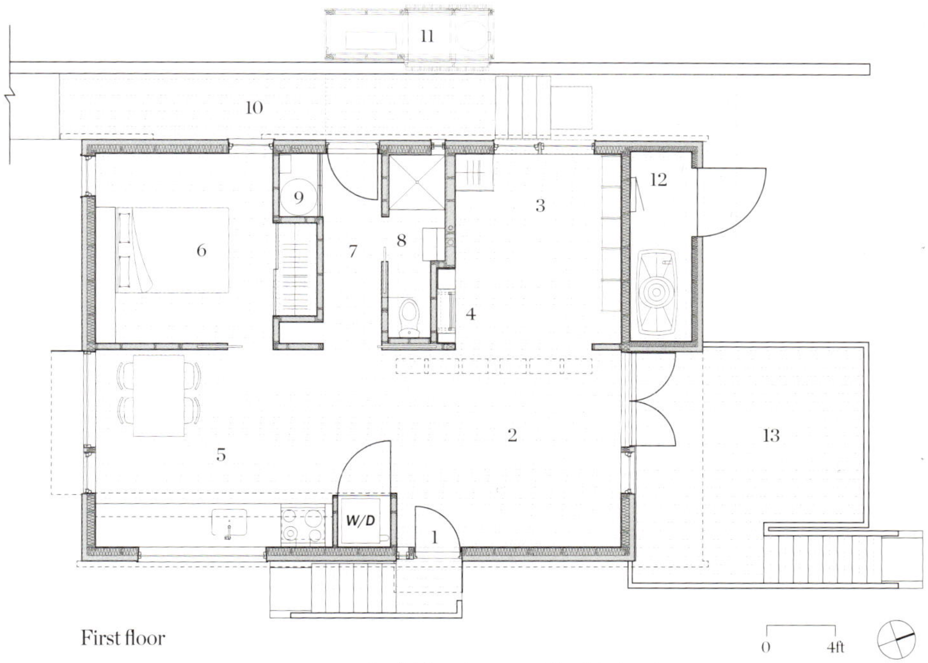

First floor

1 Public entry
2 Living
3 Swing space
4 Ladder to loft
5 Kitchen
6 Bedroom
7 Mud room
8 Bathroom
9 Mech. room
10 Private entry
11 Mech. enclosure
12 Cistern room
13 Back deck
14 Loft
15 Ventilation shutter
16 Library
17 Skylight above

Neal Prince Studio

Paw Paw Point

Sunset, South Carolina

Sited on the cusp of a lakefront knob, this shingle-style home anchors a location where dramatic open-water views across the expanse of Lake Keowee cede to the sheltering enclosure of a tranquil cove. The home is divided among three floors arranged to frame views from each living space. Inside, five bedroom suites, an open great room, kitchen, game room, and observatory accommodate comfortable family gatherings at various scales. Fireplace-equipped screen porches are connected by a covered promenade and encourage outdoor living. Cedar shingles and native fieldstone provide a warm natural palette that roots the home into its site.

The narrow, sloping, and irregularly shaped lakefront site imposed many restrictions on the home, given its sizable building program. Once the lakefront setback requirement was taken into account, only a sliver of land remained. In order to stabilize the shoreline, the owners gave up another 3 meters (10 feet) along one exposure—further reducing the buildable area. To fulfill the owners' wishes, the home would ultimately have at least seven points where it touches the various setback lines. Into this labyrinth of physical constraints came the charge: design a home that captures as many views as the site has to offer.

The organization of the home is guided by the unique qualities and constraints of the hillside, lakefront site. Its plan benches into and elbows along the cove in an interconnected series of rooms and outdoor spaces, affording every room a defining point for taking in the view. On the lake exposure, a broad stone stairway greets visitors and defines the point of arrival to the home by watercraft. The resulting building form, materials, and details work within the setting, taking advantage of topography and site features that marry the house with its natural surroundings.

Sunset, South Carolina

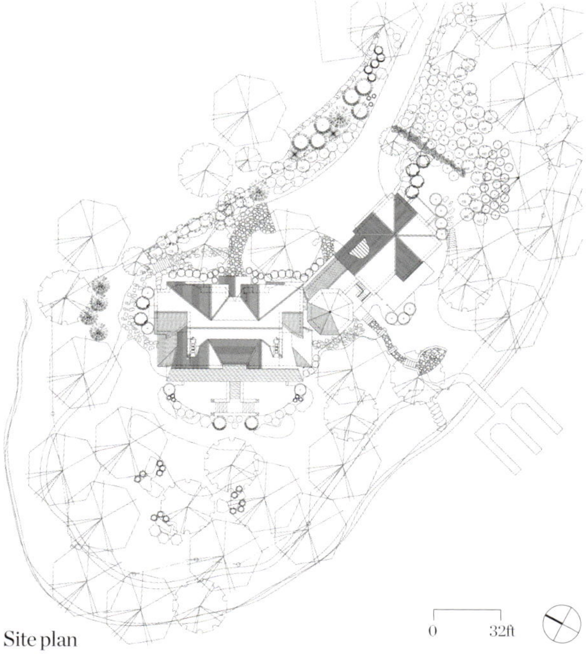

Site plan

Michael Malone Architects, Inc.

Raven Lake Ranch

Athens, Texas

It was important to the owners that the house be focused on the site and the beautiful views to the outdoors. Supporting this idea, the house has three porches, one of which is screened. This porch looks out to a mature grove of hardwoods and through them to the lakes beyond. In addition to providing shade and protection from insects, this porch is outfitted with ceiling fans and fireplace. The pattern of the screen framing matches that of the windows, truly being an outdoor room.

Containing 235 square meters (2,550 square feet) of interior area and 45 square meters (485 square feet) in screened and open porches, the house has a combined living and dining room, separated from a sitting area by a serving bar. Additionally, there are two bedrooms: the master with large bath and closet/dressing room, the other for guests with ensuite bath. Organized as an elongated, linear plan, most rooms have natural light from two and in many cases three sides. Sited at the edge of an open pasture, at the place where a grove with mature hardwoods begins, the house is the divider between field and forest. Entering from the lower roofed porches brings you into the high-ceilinged, contiguous space of the living, dining, and sitting rooms, all open through a wall of windows to views into the grove. This space is defined by a large single slope roof that contains and organizes the public spaces. The high volumes of this space, combined with the large windows, make the house seem more expansive than its compact footprint would suggest. Opening off this space, tucked under a lower ceiling are the kitchen, baths, and utility rooms, which form a contrasting edge to the higher ceilinged space.

The house is clad in two primary materials—concrete block and galvalume roofing—which extend down from the roof on some portions of the house as metal siding. The roofing material is galvalume metal; wall surfaces are concrete blocks laid in an offset running bond, with the horizontal joints tooled deeply and the vertical joints struck flush. In keeping with the simple, almost industrial palette of materials, concrete steps and terraces extend the house into the landscape. The overall gray color palette creates a contrasting backdrop to accent the bright green of the trees and pastures. Use of the concrete block and galvalume metal recall other rural structures in the area, though not traditionally for use in the construction of single family homes. Both these materials were selected for their durability and low maintenance, essentially requiring no ongoing care to remain fresh and serviceable. Tongue-and-groove cypress planks are used for the soffits of the house and at the entry porch to bring a warmer, softer texture to places where people come in tactile contact with the house.

Jan Gleysteen Architects, Inc.

Seaside Refresher

New Seabury, Massachusetts

The renovation of this waterfront home exemplifies the substantial impact of modest additions. Built in 1985, the structure was modern in detail but lacking the elegance and drama of its oceanside setting. Although the family had grown accustomed to the narrow entry, crowded courtyard, and underwhelming family room, they could not overlook the toll the ocean weather was taking on the home. Therefore aesthetic, functional, and structural improvements were addressed simultaneously in this addition/renovation project. The home's proximity to the environmentally sensitive waterfront meant the new design would work largely within the existing footprint and require less than 19 square meters (200 square feet) to be added.

The most visible improvement to the exterior is the addition of a series of gable roofs to reflect the shingle style of the Cape Cod community while improving the interior functionality. The new family room gable allowed the design team to retro-fit a steel frame to better support the vaulted room against strong and variable ocean winds. The resulting design allows for a dramatic yet elegant family room with stunning ocean views. The oceanfront setting is the visual and emotional draw for this home. However, the nearby shoreline and a modest lot required minimizing impervious surfaces. The existing gravel driveway was refurbished with a crushed oyster shell surface to allow rainwater to naturally recharge the groundwater. A 45-centimeter (18 inch) drainage strip, also covered with crushed oyster shell, runs along the perimeter of the house reducing the impact of roof runoff. Native plantings soften the landscape with low maintenance and minimal watering.

Physical limitations were also a driving factor for the addition/renovation. The narrow entry hall is located off a tight courtyard between the main house and guest house. Any design that widened the entry hall could, in turn, exacerbate an already cramped courtyard. The solution was to borrow 1.5 meters (5 feet) from the courtyard and replace the existing stair with an open design paired with a vaulted ceiling made possible by a new gable roof. In the courtyard, smaller scaled native plantings and a new bluestone patio revitalized the overgrown courtyard.

The gable additions aimed at solving the home's functional and structural deficiencies provided an opportunity to update the exterior aesthetic of the home. Updated details and window grilles bring scale to the exterior massing, while pergolas help define arrival areas and bridge the gap between the main and guest houses. To better protect the home from the oceanside environment, wood trim and decking were replaced with synthetic materials. New pergolas were locally fabricated from extruded PVC. Ocean-facing windows were replaced with hurricane-rated glass. UV film was added to prevent heat gain and fading of the interior finishes. The new structural steel frame in the family room is complemented by a laminated ring beam supporting the new tower, to provide a stable, yet responsive structure.

Front elevation

Rear elevation

Joeb Moore + Partners Architects

Spiral House

Old Greenwich, Connecticut, USA

Situated along the Connecticut shoreline of Long Island Sound, the Spiral House seeks to engage, enhance, and reflect its situation, responding to the conditions of light, air, and water specific to the coastal climate. The building mass and envelope are a direct outcome of the application of the strict local environmental and zoning regulations, which prescribe flood elevations, building height, setbacks, and footprint. The spatial organization is based on a spiral, employed as a metaphor for nature and organic growth and serving to intertwine and elegantly entangle the socio-spatial roles of the program and the interior and exterior spaces, blurring the limits between house and context.

From a sculpted concrete plinth rises a spiral, wooden, finned structure that contains and screens a transparent box of floor-to-floor glass curtain walls. The plinth lifts the entire volume above the 4.3-meter (14 feet) flood level, extending an entry ramp through a water containment garden. A steel-and-glass "box" of 3.4-meter tall (11 feet) frameless doors and windows sits safely atop the blade like slab, affording extraordinary views of Long Island Sound, a mere 10 meters (35 feet) away.

The wood spiral moves around and above the glass room, employing vertical red cedar fined cladding to unify the unique programs and elevations, while allowing variation and exception in transparency. Responding to both program and site, it works to maximize privacy and view simultaneously. Its material was selected as a way of innovating upon the traditional cedar shingle and clapboard houses in the surrounding neighborhood. Together, the floating base, the lightweight spiral structure, and the play of transparencies and reflections of the skin produce a complex range of shifting perceptions that enhance the relationship between the house and its coastal location.

Adding to the interdependence of house and landscape, the spiral also functions as an ecological loop, funneling rainwater from the roof and terraces through the entry water garden. Water is collected in a cistern located at the base of the house's vortex, or central vertical gap. The garden slowly filters the water until it reaches the high-level invert and then releases it back into the Long Island Sound.

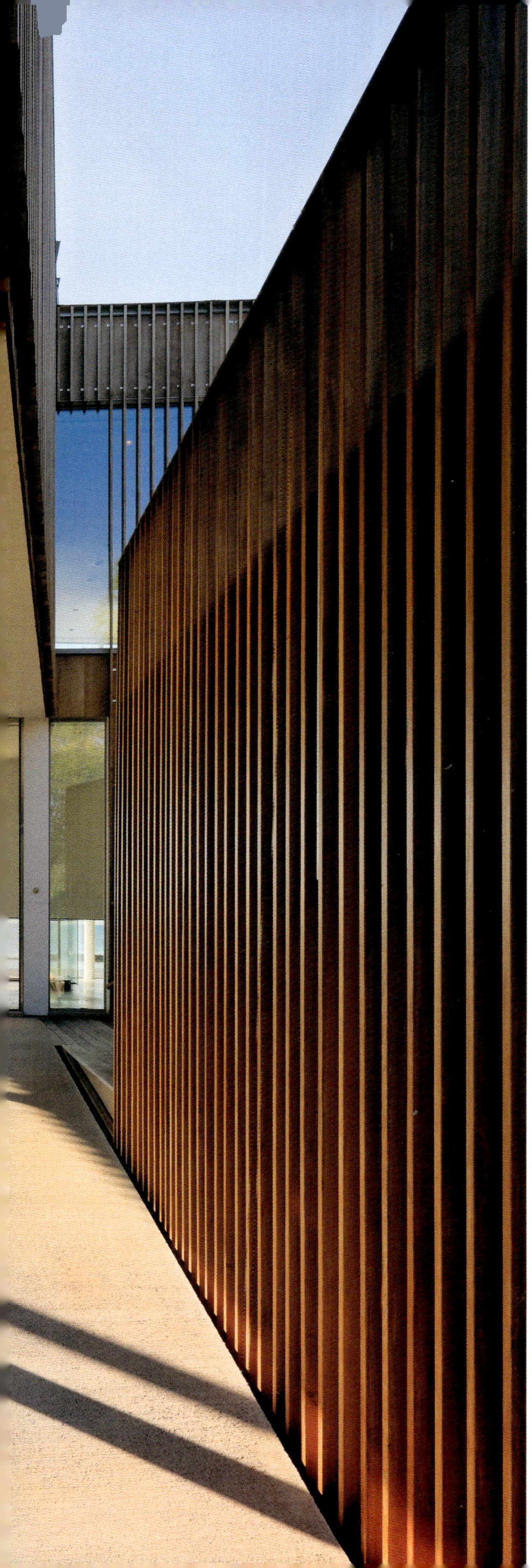

Ronnette Riley Architect

Westside Townhouse

New York City, New York

The Upper West Side of New York City is a vibrant, diverse community known for its current and past residents. It spans from Riverside Park on the west to Central Park on the east. Actors, entrepreneurs, and longtime locals mix and mingle in the street cafes. Residents stroll and bike along the Hudson River and throughout Olmstead's iconic park.

The Upper West Side has a rich heritage of residential townhouses. They are multi-story dwellings that can be identified by their ornately carved stone façades, significant stoops, and grand double leaf entrance doors. Most are over 100 years old and in need of restoration and new infrastructure to sustain their presence through another century. This Westside Townhouse dates back to 1885. The client chose it for its convenient location and development potential. The program goal was to create a family retreat that balanced community living and privacy. The architectural goal was to open up the space to additional light and air and at the same time preserve the architectural heritage.

Ronnette Riley Architect (RRA) worked with the client to develop the most desirable program, given the zoning and building constraints. It was designed to have six bedroom suites located on varying floors. The kitchen, dining room, living room, and parlor on the lower floors are shared. Storage, laundry, and a wine cellar reside in the basement and cellar. A new studio apartment on the ground floor accommodates a caretaker. In order to accomplish the spatial requirements, the building was gutted and a cellar excavated under the existing structure. The floors and stairs were re-built and a roof top deck, with serving amenities, was incorporated to allow for enjoyment of the surrounding roofscape and vistas.

RRA worked closely with the NYC Landmarks Commission to restore the historical character of the building and neighborhood. RRA developed the design based on research of historical photos and period details. A new stoop and new double-leaf entry doors were designed to mimic the original. Reclaimed brick was used on the rear addition to replicate the patina of the original construction. A decorative metal cornice was repaired and restored with a new wrought iron guardrail to crown the building. The rear of the building was opened up to enhance solar gain and ventilation with full height steel frame windows. The plan was carefully worked to incorporate new HVAC, elevator, and electrical systems.

A winding staircase rises six stories through the home that serves as the connecting element and a source of natural ventilation and shared light. A delicate interplay of Victorian millwork detailing at the openings, cove, and base of the rooms reflects the same period restoration design as on the exterior. Although committed to the traditional theming, RRA took liberties with the selection of colors, finishes, and fixtures that worked with the client's preferences.

NYPD

Tropical/Sub-Tropical

Hot and humid in low-lying areas, slightly cooler and drier in higher areas, this region is generally dry, but prolonged rainy seasons may occur. High temperatures and humidity are persistent, particularly enervating closer to the Equator. The architecture needs to take into account the possibility of heavy prolonged rain and high humidity.

Terceira Quarterly Associates
Ariel Sands - The Villas

Ariel Sands, Devonshire Parish, Bermuda

The requirement was to design a unique and luxurious villa development for Ariel Sands, a Boutique Cottage Colony Resort, as phase one of a master plan to redevelop the entire resort. The challenge was to overcome a difficult hillside site and to create a lush and private setting, while preserving water views for each villa. The proposed Hotel Sargasso Sea Spa became one of the sources of inspiration for the villas.

The design of the villas is inspired by the earliest Bermuda vernacular architecture and the concept of a coastal spa lifestyle. The exterior architecture derived from the pure forms of stepped gables, buttery roofs, and barrel-vaulted water tanks seen in examples of Bermuda's oldest buildings. All ornamentation is omitted and the strong simple white volumes are composed to allow light and shadow to reveal sculptural beauty in the landscape. The intention was to create a design that is modern in spirit with deep historical reference.

The strong and simple volumes of the exterior massing are expressed on the interior as grand spaces with beamed cathedral and vaulted ceilings opening onto gracious terraces, a pool house and infinity edge plunge pool with ocean views. The exterior of the villas have a distinctly modern and Mediterranean feel. Each villa is composed of the same elements reconfigured to suite each site and is fully landscaped with a unique garden inspired by "The Tempest", a play by William Shakespeare (said to be set in Bermuda), from which Ariel Sands derives its name.

The finishes and fixtures of the villas have all been chosen for their sensual qualities: fossilized limestone, coconut palm, and lava rock, which resonate with the qualities of the volcanic coral island of Bermuda and the vibrant ocean waters of the Sargasso Sea. The recent development of commercially available home spa fixtures like the Sok tub and the hydrotherapy shower from Kohler make the private home spa possible.

The spa lifestyle is reflected in a devotion to wellness and adherence to Feng Shui design principles. The informal and gracious open-plan design, meditation pavilion, and sleeping porch with shutters and chaise lounges all promote casual living. In the master suite, custom-designed private indoor and outdoor spa rooms with chaise lounge and treatment bench promise sanctuary and balance. Villa residents may receive spa treatments, ordered through the Sargasso Sea Spa, in their own private spa room.

The villas have been designed to be a delight for the senses and a sanctuary for the soul, rich with meaning and a deep connection to the history of Bermuda and the mysterious powers of the ocean. The Villas have already been voted as one of the top 50 luxuries in Bermuda by the *Bermuda Homes & Gardens* magazine. An actor/producer was the first to purchase a unit, of which Terceira Quarterly Associates completed the interior design as shown in the interior images.

Ariel Sands, Devonshire Parish, Bermuda

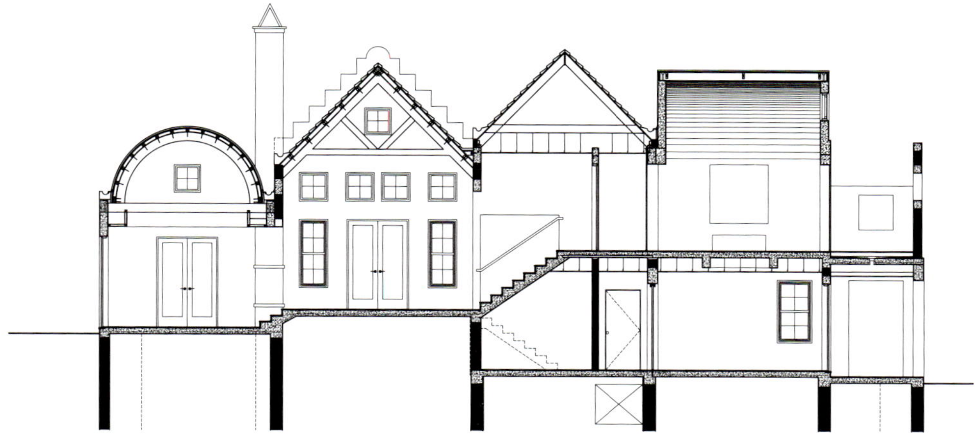

First floor

1 Entry gate
2 Forecourt
3 Foyer
4 Great room with beamed cathedral ceiling over lounge and vaulted ceiling over dining and kitchen area
5 Laundry/pantry
6 Garage
7 Terrace with bamboo pergola and infinity edge plunge pool
8 Pool house with BBQ
9 Sunken garden with gate and pathway to private beach
10 Bedroom
11 Den/bedroom
12 Covered porch

Frederick + Frederick Architects

Contemporary Dogtrot

Beaufort County, South Carolina

The clients desired a sustainable retreat that maximized the views on their barrier island waterfront lot. The architect turned to the vernacular dogtrot form to reduce the amount of conditioned space, while creating comfortable outdoor living. In dogtrots, also known as "two pens and a passage," one room was typically used for sleeping and the other for cooking. The open center passage was the main sitting area that was cooled naturally by the Bernoulli effect. In this contemporary dogtrot, the center hall is the foyer and sitting room. There is a perforated wall and door on the front and a folding perforated wall on the rear that can be closed and locked for security. The master bedroom suite is to the east of the center passage with the great room to the west.

The large terrace is curved around a live oak tree, with a lap pool and spa centered on the entry, which immediately connects you to the specialness of this place. The porch with retractable screens is angled to capture the long view down the river. The boardwalk encircles the terrace to break the distance to grade and thus eliminates the need for guardrails. Through the use of folding walls the house seamlessly transitions from inside to outside. The light-filled great room has operable windows and transoms for great cross ventilation. The south-facing windows are protected by the bracketed overhang that is designed to block the summer solstice sun.

Other sustainable strategies include a reflective "cool roof," cypress reverse board and batten siding, river-recovered cypress ceilings, low-e impact resistant glass, cellulose foam insulation, a conditioned crawl space, reclaimed heart pine floors, super high-efficiency heat pump with an energy recovery ventilator, instantaneous water heaters, three-form cabinet inserts, and low VOC paint and finishes. This private retreat connects a young family to the joys of nature and the bounty of the sea.

Floor plan

SCDA Architects

Grange Road House II

Singapore

Grange Road House II is located on a steeply sloped site in central Singapore. The architectural form of the house is a composition of two elongated rectangular volumes, sensitively integrated into the terrain and carefully planned to enhance two tall existing conservation trees—each more than a century old. The volumes project out dramatically over the zones, and work together to emphasise the surrounding natural qualities.

Entry to the house is through a gently sloped granite-clad driveway that leads to the base of a ramp where a generous car porch lined with a stone feature wall, an extensive aluminum trellis ceiling, and a copper-and-glass sculpture await. Upon passing the feature wall, a monotone finished foyer is revealed, here another sculpture in the form of a 7-meter (23 feet) copper tree greets visitors on arrival. Here, repetitive finishes augment both the sculpture and the occupants, emphasizing the artwork and surrounding activities against a condensed backdrop.

Each level of the two volumes is imbued with a different character; the more public first-floor level is clad in a light-colored granite finish in a variety of textures, while the private upper-second-floor level is clothed in bone-white aluminum panels. Connecting the two parallel volumes is a transparent glass-lined transition corridor that complements and links circulation between both ends.

The distinctive feature of the design is the set of two cantilevered rectangular volumes. Both offer panoramic views out to the city and accentuate the location of the house where it is perched on the peak of the immediate hill. The cantilevered volumes bring the occupants closer to the natural features of the site, and windows are positioned to address the conservation trees and invite views of nature into the house, creating a vital relationship between inside and outside. The result is primarily a response to the unique site qualities, and reflects the intent to craft a house that translates simplicity of volumes and lines, addressing the demanding, yet picturesque of the locale.

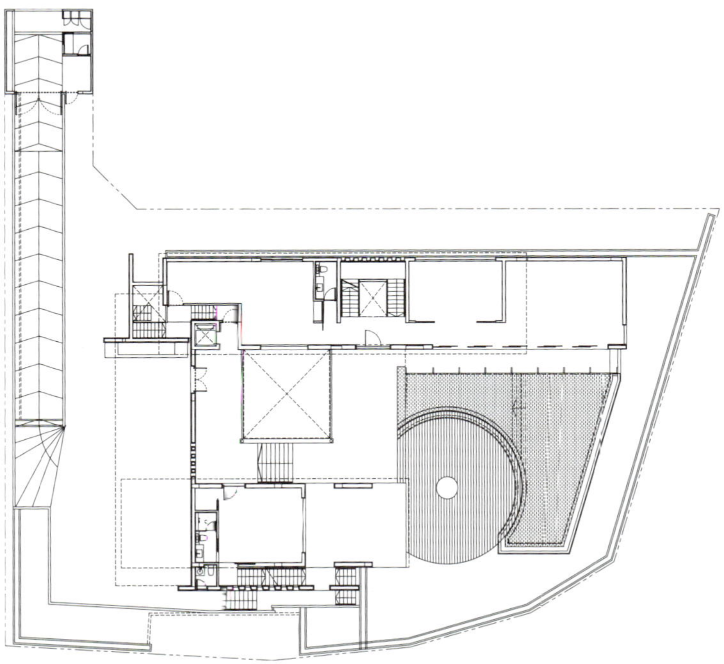

First floor

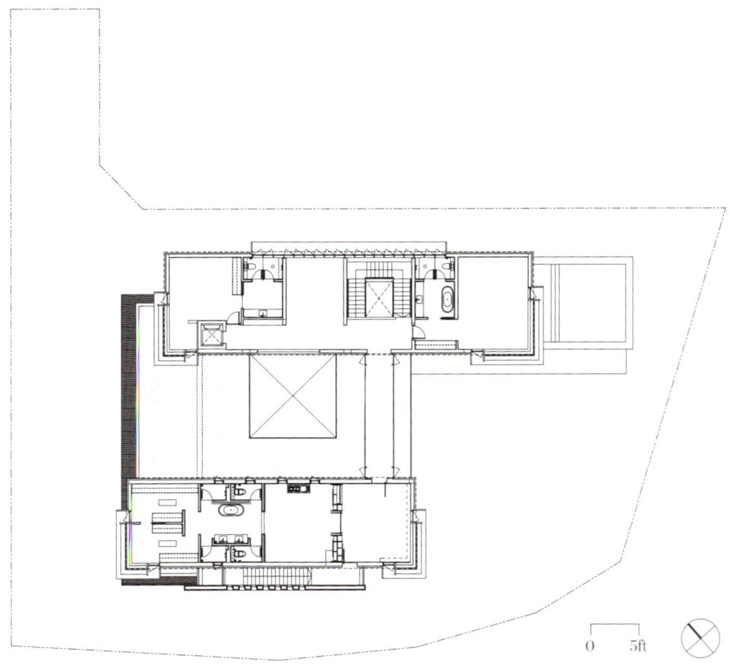

Second floor

Robert A.M. Stern Architects

House at Seaside

Seaside, Florida

This small 250-square meter (2,700 square feet) house located on the water at Seaside, Florida, combines high style classical wooden detailing in the vocabulary popular at turn-of-the-century seaside resorts. The design challenge was to find a unique and individual architectural expression suitable to seaside living within the tight codes that Seaside provides for each lot. The house is meant to fit into the beachside community and yet to raise the bar for future Seaside houses with a knowledgeable reinterpretation of classical detailing typical of older houses. The relatively modest structure is iconic by virtue of the theme of the offset stacked columns and pilasters, which, combined with cedar pergolas and copper roofs, recalls the mannerist compositions of 1920s Nordic architecture.

The design of this oceanfront house in the influential New Urbanist planned town of Seaside, Florida, adheres to the town's strict code requirements for its particular lot, yet is subtly unique. Its design combines the elegance of 1930s Swedish Classicism with the charming vernacular of turn-of-the-century wooden American seaside resort houses. The compact plan looks to the traditional urban townhouse model but employs a side entry through the garden.

Children's bedrooms are located at the garden level, with the great room at the piano nobile, both with porches overlooking the ocean. The master bedroom suite, with sweeping vistas of both the town and the ocean, occupies the third level. The master bedroom's over-sized windows take advantage of the dramatic view of the Gulf. The single iconic Ionic column supports a pergola and provides sweeping diagonal views of the beach. The living room porch provides an area for outdoor gathering and dining. The columns, handrails, ceiling beaming, and lantern carry the classical detailing to the porch frame the spectacular ocean view. The interior architecture continues the simplified wooden Classicism consistent with the exterior design.

The west façade, which faces the town, employs superimposed orders to create a public scale. The oceanside porches are organized with stacked orders of fluted and inscribed Greek columns in antis culminating in a trussed and trellised roof supported by a single Ionic column, which gives the house an iconic identity from the beach. The siding at the lower level is rusticated wood meant to imitate stone, rising up to beveled clapboard at the upper levels, which culminates in a batten copper roof and an open rafter eave embellished with decorative caps. The overall effect is a balance of naivete and sophistication. Characterized by its Swedish Classical 'Gustavian' color scheme, the sunny shades of blue and yellow are reminiscent of the sea and sky. The interiors reflect the sense of being on a ship, with built-in alcove seats and beds throughout. Furniture design inspiration ranges from Neo-Grec to classic wicker, and the screened-in porch features a daybed-variation of the traditional porch-swing.

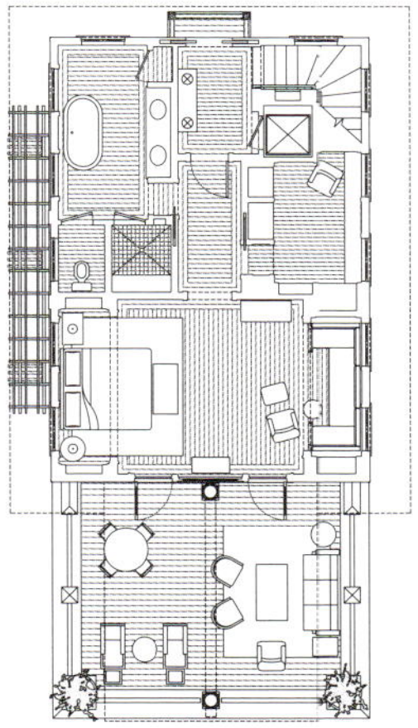

Third floor

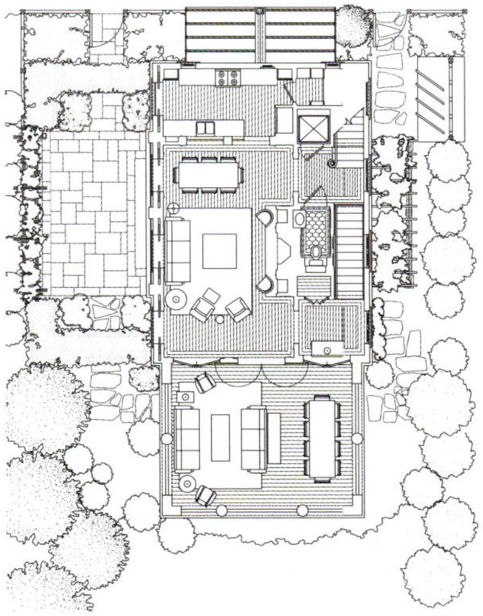

Second floor

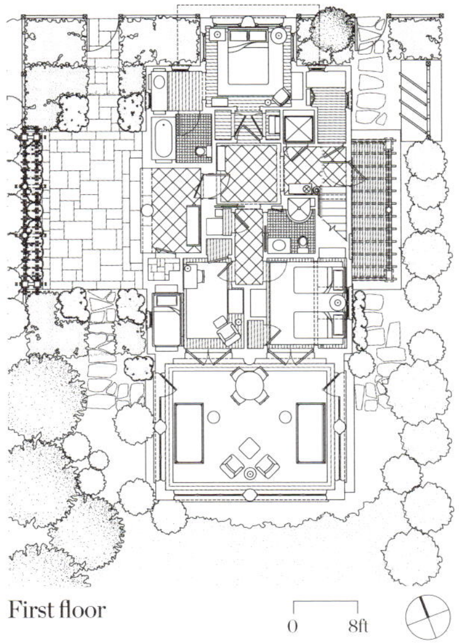

First floor

Duvall Decker Architects

Oak Ridge House

Jackson, Mississippi

Home is not just a place, but a process of locating ourselves in public and in nature. There are times we seek envelopment inside boundaries, for physical and psychological security. There are times we seek exposure and risk. It enlivens us. We move between these spatial poles, never purely in one state or the other. Envelopment is a retreat into the comfort of interior boundaries. Exposure is a circumstance of risk, an insecurity that leads to boundlessness and creative freedom.

A challenging home is a scaffold for this field of potential experiences, creating opportunities to move between these conditions, to inhabit and interpret each of them over time. More than a house, it is a plural physiological position, at once secure and comfortable, and at risk, open to individual creative freedom. In this open and evolving process, balance is neither possible nor desired. We strive to grow in this field of experience, sometimes from a position of risk, other times from a secure posture, often from somewhere in between.

The house is located in a post-World War II neighborhood and the lot backs up to the oak-lined ridge for which the street is named. The site, 30 meters (100 feet) wide and 75 meters (245 feet) deep, slopes 3.7 meters (12 feet) up from street to ridge. The east–west oriented site is ideal for solar access and for the variety of light available to animate the interior of the house over the course of a day and through the seasons. The southern, inner city street is lush with trees and flowering plants.

The 350-square meter (3,750 square feet) Oak Ridge House is a composition of intertwined volumes, shapes, and spaces. An open living/dining room, and a long rectangular private bedroom wing interpenetrate to form the kitchen. The large open room is pushed toward a condition of exposure, with a curtainwall to the east and a band of shaded windows to the west. This tall volume feels more like an open courtyard than an interior. The north and south walls of the large room are more like building façades than interior partitions. The south wall/façade is a continuation of the exterior wall of the south wing that penetrates into the living/dining room. The north wall/façade screens the loft and lower studio with a pecan-paneled bookcase/stair and a concrete wall/stair that grows out of the lower studio. With the drapes open and the right light, the public view from the street pushes through the house and into the private yard. At other times, the space feels like an extension of the private yard. Glass subdivides interior and exterior, acting as both veil and mirror, constantly doubling inside out, outside in. The boundaries of space are indeterminate, alive, and negotiable. These expansions and interpenetrations soften the boundary of the room, fostering a constant invitation for measurement and negotiation.

4044

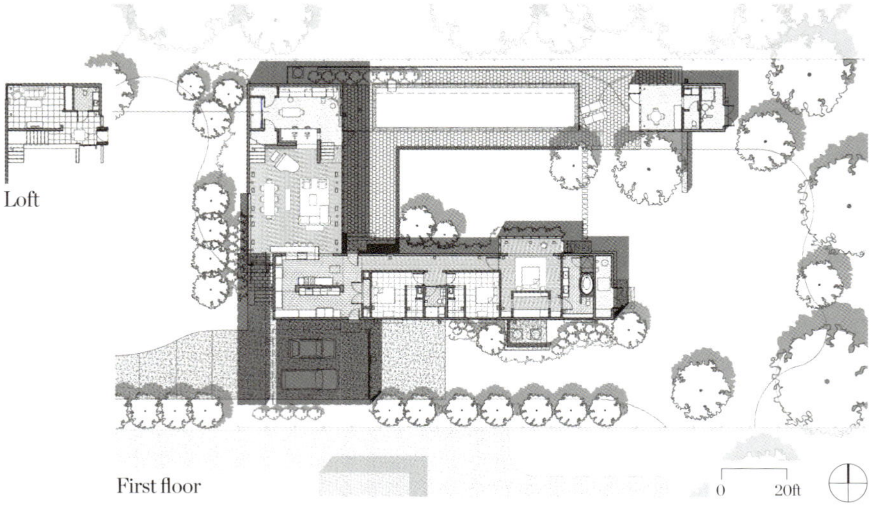
Loft
First floor
0
20ft

DETAIL

Arid/Semi-Arid

Seasons run the gamut from hot-dry and hot-humid to winter and various transitional conditions. What differentiates this climate region is that moisture in the form of rain, humidity, and snow may be short lived. Architectural responses take into account prolonged sun exposure, lack of moisture and natural ventilation. While this is true for all climate regions, in the arid/semi-arid regions these factors predominate.

Interface Architects

1600 City Lights

Santa Fe, New Mexico

The semi-arid region encompassing New Mexico, having essentially no indigenous industry, has long been economically depressed. A century ago, the new state's governor William McDonald determined that establishing the state as a unique tourist destination would provide a sorely-needed economic base. To accomplish this, building style constraints based on ancient Anasazi archetypes such as the Taos pueblo were instituted, and survive to this day. Santa Fe in particular became known as a city of low-profile, flat-roofed, earth-toned adobe buildings--often with protruding vigas casting their characteristic shadows. A contemporary variant of that archetype is generally known as the "Santa Fe style."

1600 City Lights is a carefully crafted interpretation of that style, thus reflecting indirectly the historic, cultural, climatic, and environmental imperitives of the region. The salient aspects of this home include earth-toned stucco walls with minimal openings, save for a pair of large glazed sliders providing access to the spectacular views of the City and surrounding mountains. The building profile is kept low, in accordance with not only the regional norms, but also severe height limitations imposed by the subdivision covenants.

The residence is sited on challenging topography, which is sloping and convoluted. Subdivision covenants require floor levels to follow the slopes closely, usually resulting in numerous interior levels. However, by substantially depressing the uphill floor plate of the building, over 80 per cent of the main living floor is preserved as a single, stepless level—providing residents with the prospect of comfortably "aging in place."

The linear, bi-axial plan is centrally anchored by a stone chimney mass, which supports two fireplaces, as well as the entry water feature. The pair of pocketed, zero-threshold glazed sliders—facing east and north—are shaded by the semi-circular portal roof. In season, these sliders can entirely disappear, resulting in a completely uninterrupted spatial flow between the interior and sheltered exterior living spaces.

Among the major environmental concerns in the region (intense sun, flash flooding, episodic wildfires), the most crucial is the harvesting and conservation of water. To this end, this home employs a 17,000-liter (4,500 gallons) sub-grade cistern to capture roof stormwater runoff. The xeric landscaping is maintained by automatic drip irrigation, fed by the cistern. The building's passive ventilation system features operable windows, clerestories and insulated skylights.

The highly insulated roof is sheathed with a UV-resistant, light-colored TPO membrane for reduced heat gain. A portion of the roof is fitted with a 3.2-kW array of photovoltaic solar collection modules to provide most of the electrical energy needs of the household. Through careful attention to orientation, material and appliance selection, and energy-conscious detailing, the home has been certified by the USGBC with a LEED Silver rating.

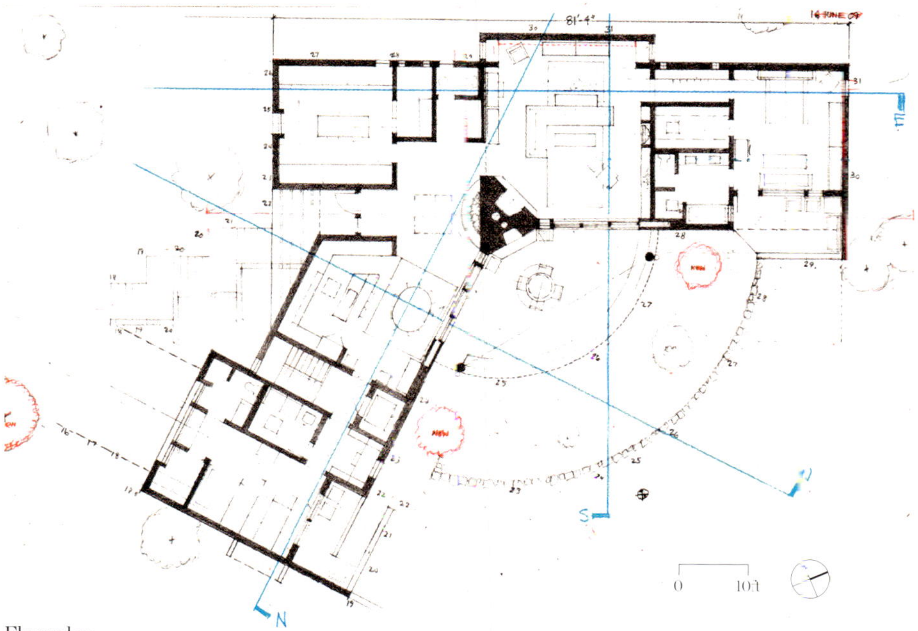

Floor plan

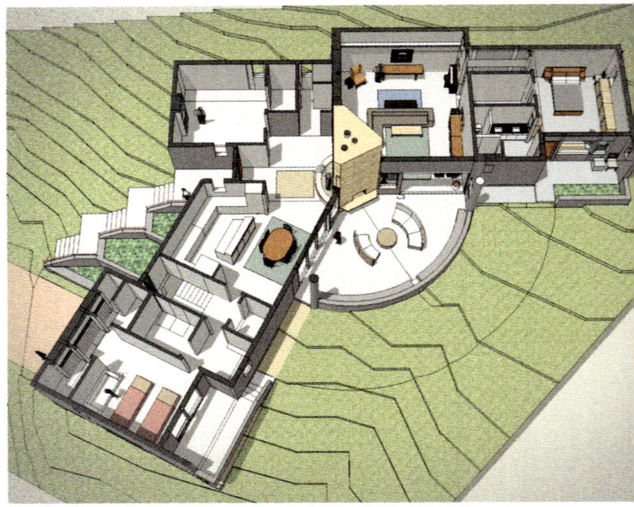

NAGA

Al Ghurair

Dubai

Hidden behind a circular drive and a curving screen wall, the Al Gurair residence reveals itself in stages. At 1,265 square meters (13,616 square feet), the residence is organized on a single level that gracefully offers both intimate family spaces and a panoramic view of the grounds—including pools, terraces, and two massive Cubist sculptures, all connected to the main building by a dramatic pilaster-edged pathway. Through the use of natural stone, the entire residence carries an ambiance of warmth and luxury.

This theme continues outdoors with shallow reflection pools and gardens. The interior carries the same warmth by utilizing an identical palette of materials but in finer articulation.

The house uses a conventional forced air conditioning system but the exterior walls are mostly solid and thick, in order to act as thermal masses to help reduce heat gain. Additionally, each bedroom uses a second exterior wall for shading as well as privacy. The glazing is strategically located at the entry and surrounding the courtyard, to provide passive cooling effects, especially in the summer.

1 Entrance
2 Majlis
3 Formal dining room
4 Living room
5 Family dining room
6 Kitchen
7 Bedroom
8 Sitting area
9 Master bedroom
10 Master dresser
11 Master bathroom
12 Maid's living
13 Maid's room
14 Storage
15 Informal majlis

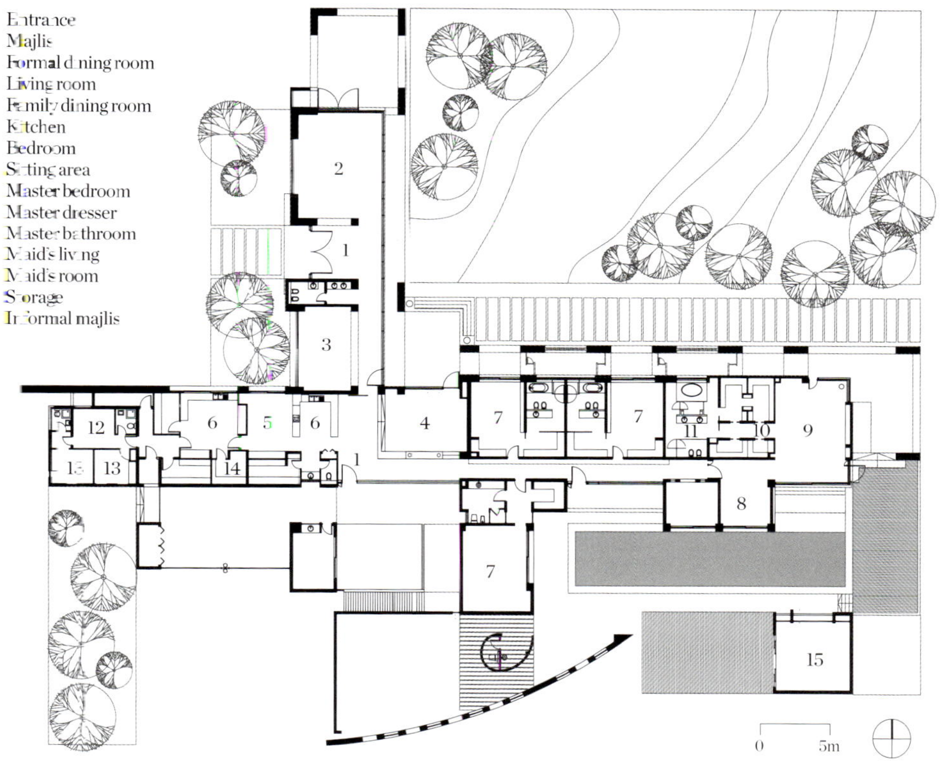

Studio 9one2 Architecture

Galloro Lull Vacation House

Punta Colorada, Baja, Mexico

This modest scale vacation home was built entirely by local labor, using local building techniques. Very little—84 square meters (900 square feet)—of the house is heated or cooled. Most is semi-open to the outdoors due to the very consistent air temperatures year round.

The primary concept was to create a controlled environment through a courtyard scheme with a fresh water plunge, breaking the scale of the building down into a single story pavilion and a two story pavilion, thus providing an outdoor living space centrally located and protected from the elements.

The all-concrete structure, which was hand-mixed at the site, is very stingy with regard to utilizing few natural resources to construct. Even the sand spoils from the homes foundations were used in the mixing of the concrete.

Located in Baja on the Sea of Cortez, this home is near a small village, in an area known for pristine game fishing.

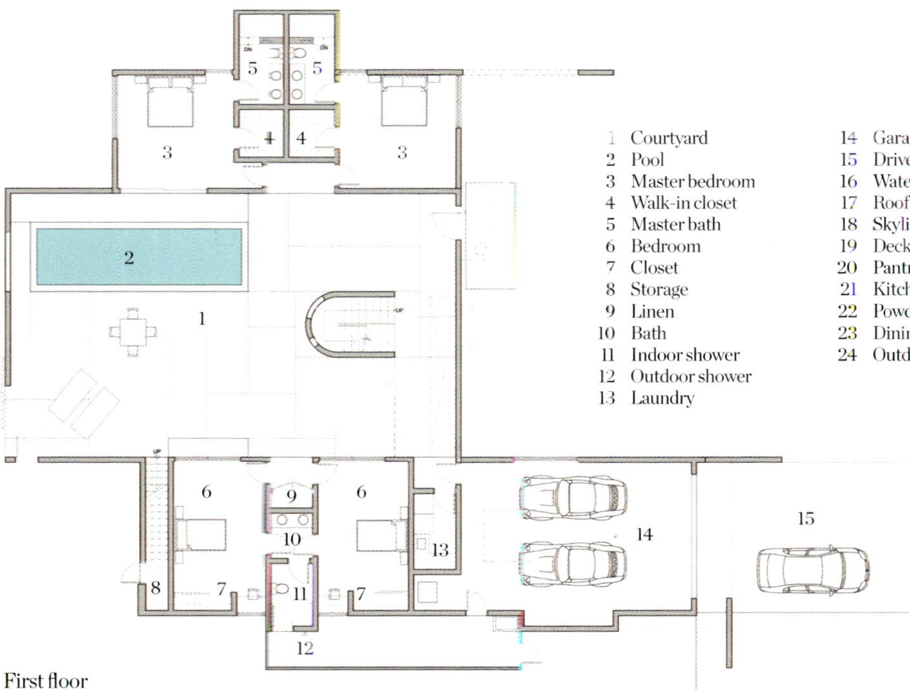

First floor

1 Courtyard
2 Pool
3 Master bedroom
4 Walk-in closet
5 Master bath
6 Bedroom
7 Closet
8 Storage
9 Linen
10 Bath
11 Indoor shower
12 Outdoor shower
13 Laundry
14 Garage
15 Driveway
16 Water feature
17 Roof
18 Skylight
19 Deck
20 Pantry
21 Kitchen
22 Powder room
23 Dining area
24 Outdoor living area

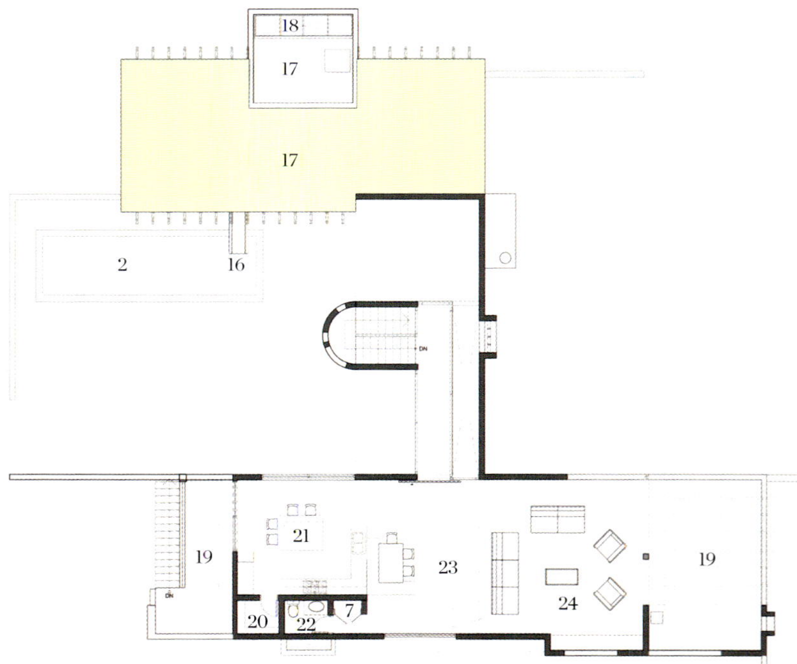

Second floor

0 3ft

Lloyd & Associates Architects

Monte Sereno House

Santa Fe, New Mexico

The owner requested a southwest contemporary design that was compatible with Santa Fe contemporary design, while meeting the architectural covenants of the subdivision. The owner also wanted an efficient and functional floor plan to be as environmentally sensitive as the building budget would allow. The house sets comfortably on the relatively flat portion of the site, a few feet from the outdoor terraces running continuously along the east facade. The site slopes down more than 30 per cent. The Sangre de Cristo Mountains are visible to the east. The north wall is bermed into the side of the hill, making the floor level 2 meters (7 feet) below grade. The west and front of the house face the street. There is no "long hallway," so the circulation becomes part of the room. When you enter the foyer you are greeted by a subtle wall-flowing fountain, which divides the entry from the main living area. As you move around this wall it opens to a commanding mountain view.

Every wall in the house has a glass wall to the east to take full advantage of the stunning mountain views. All rooms are set-up along a very thick north-south wall that runs the entire length of the house. This wall not only allows windows to be deep set but provides open shelves to some rooms, cabinets at the dining area and duct work for the cooling system. The house is "wall dominant," a flat-roofed contemporary rendition of Pueblo or Santa Fe Style that is the vernacular in New Mexico. The western sunsets can be observed by climbing the exterior stairs to a rooftop deck.

The house achieved a 43 hers (Home Energy Rating System) rating. The walls are built of Rastra, which is recycled styrofoam mixed with concrete which provides an R-40 wall when poured 30 centimeters (12 inches) thick. There is no formaldehyde in any of the building materials. The radiant floor heat is supplied by thermal solar collectors mounted vertically all along the south wall and backed up by a natural gas boiler. There are photovoltaic collectors on the garage roof at a very low angle, so they are completely concealed from view.

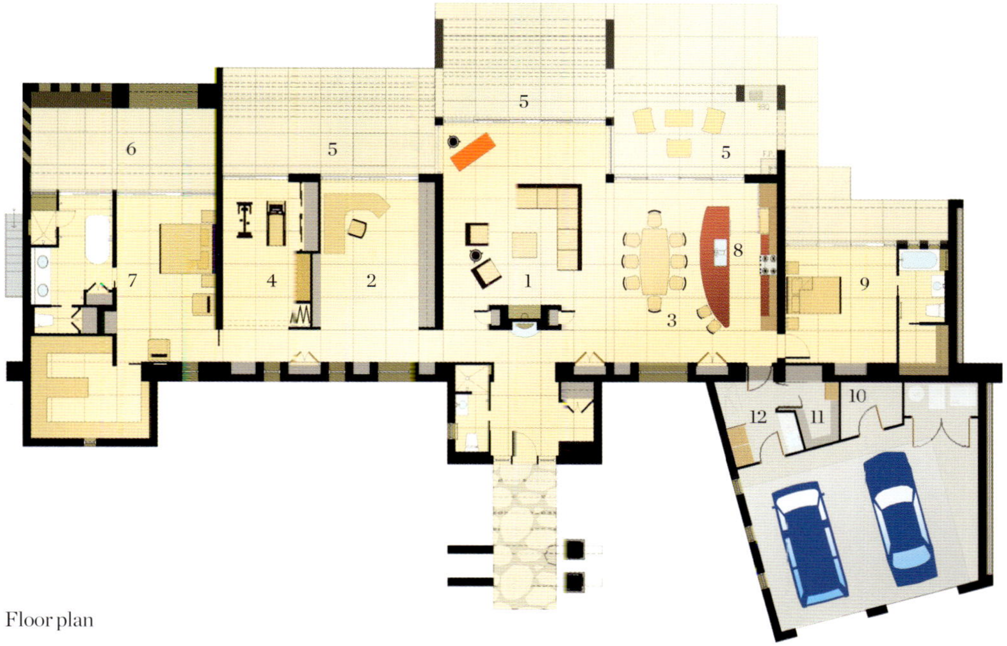

1 Living
2 Office
3 Dining
4 Exercise
5 Terrace
6 Private terrace
7 Master
8 Kitchen
9 Guest
10 Storage
11 Pantry
12 Laundry

0 8ft

Floor plan

David Hovey Jr. AIA / Optima DCHGlobal Inc.

Relic Rock

Scottsdale, Arizona

David Hovey Jr. designed Relic Rock as the prototype for the DCHGlobal Building System, a sustainable standardized building system enabling design flexibility in horizontal and vertical directions and can be constructed quickly and efficiently in any location, climate, or terrain.

The DCHGlobal Building System is based on a 2.15-meter (7 feet) horizontal module, a 40-centimeter (15 inches) vertical module, and a 6.4-meter (21 feet) structural bay. A series of connector plates enables the assembly of C-shaped beams and column angles to form a 3-dimensional structural grid, allowing all components to be standardized to facilitate automated fabrication and precise construction. Beams, columns, connectors, and plate components are connected into "assemblies" in the shop and sequentially transported to the site for fast, efficient erection. The system allows a 2.15-meter (7 feet) floor cantilever and a 4.3-meter (14 feet) roof cantilever, providing functional design flexibility and large roof overhangs for solar control. All exterior structural and architectural elements comprise Cor-Ten steel.

Relic Rock embodies the DCHGlobal Building System and synthesis of nature and technology. Located in the high Sonoran desert of Scottsdale, Arizona at the foothills of the Tonto National Forest, the extraordinary site features deep, rugged ravines, large boulder formations, and remarkable vegetation and animal life. Hovey Jr. designed Relic Rock to sit lightly on the land with elevated floors and decks that float above the desert and integrate with the unique characteristics of the site. The connection to nature is further achieved with the envelope, which comprises entirely low-E UV protected laminated glass with a heat-reflective coating, dissolving the division of interior and exterior space. Natural lighting is abundant in every room, reducing the need for electricity, reinforced by a 25-kW photovoltaic system integrated into the roof. Through the use of extensive overhangs and adjustable sunscreens, the glass is protected from the sun throughout the summer and acts as a canvas for nature's reflections of both color and texture. Cantilevered from the perimeter of the roof structure, horizontal plates are perforated with 3-centimeter (1.25 inches) holes, creating a moving dotted pattern inside and out that follows the angle of the sun and moon.

Optima DCHGlobal acts as the developer, architect, and general contractor, resulting in efficiencies of design, entitlements, permitting, and construction that cannot be realized through traditional project delivery methods. BIM software provides precise fabrication and construction coordination, accurate bidding, and 5-dimensional scheduling and construction management. Relic Rock has been granted the highest level of certification for green building by the nationally recognized City of Scottsdale Green Building Program and won the 2013 International Property World's Best Award – Best Single Family House and the 2012 AIA National Housing Award – Best Custom Home.

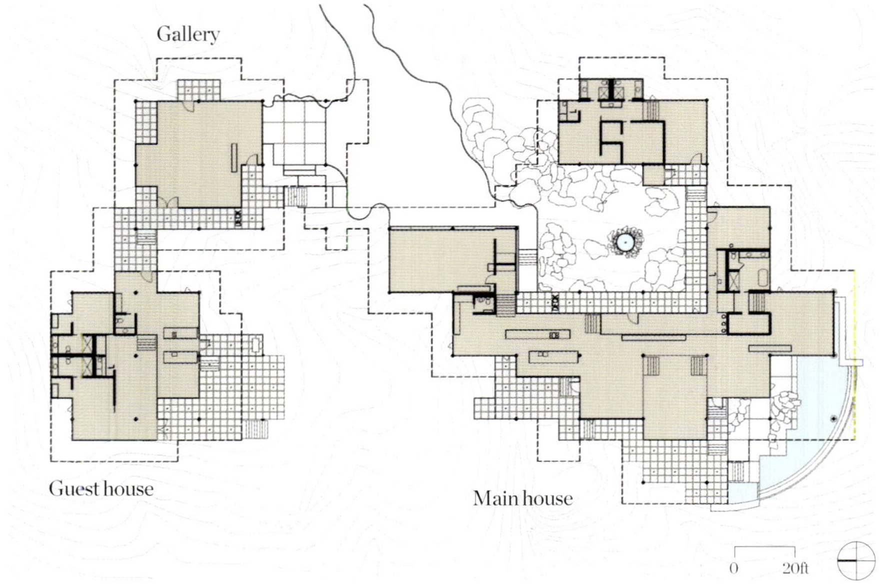
Gallery
Guest house
Main house
0
20ft

Contracts are a Thing of Beauty

By Deborah M. DeBernard, AIA, NCARB, AIBC-Architect, LEED BD+C
Vice President and General Manager, American Institute of Architects Contract Documents

Many people start a construction project, particularly a residential construction project, looking at beautiful images in magazines, searching websites or visiting remarkable built projects. Beyond showing these images and sites to your architect, there is much more communication needed to progress from the thrill of the initial design research to the finished project. The fundamental communication tool in the project toolbox is the written contract that describes what the project is and how each party is expected to perform. In a 2013 survey, most insurance experts agreed that miscommunication is a leading cause of professional liability claims. Avoiding miscommunication begins with having a well written contract.

What to Include

Even the smallest projects can benefit from the use of written contracts, but contracts do not need to be any longer or more complicated than the project dictates. Each contract should be tailored to the specifics of the project and should include a detailed project description (size, location, budget including any allowances), a scope of services, terms setting forth the responsibilities of each party, a schedule including important milestone events, terms describing how and when fees are to be paid and an explanation of the processes for changing the scope of work/services and settling disputes. Terms addressing insurance requirements, ownership of the design documents, jobsite safety or rights to terminate the work should also be considered.

No Need to Start from Scratch

For more than 100 years, The American Institute of Architects (AIA) has been providing contract documents to owners, architects and contractors for projects of all sizes, levels of complexity, construction delivery methods (i.e. design-bid-build, design-build) and budgets. Each contract is carefully written to provide a balanced position for owners, architects and contractors. Additionally, the parties can have confidence that the terms of each contract are coordinated with the other AIA contracts used on the project, contain no gaps in responsibilities, cover risks that are often overlooked in other contracts, and are helpful for coordinating the activities of each party. More information about these contracts can be obtained at www.aia.org/contractdocs

Using a Contract Successfully

At the beginning of most projects, it is easy to find agreement between all parties involved in the design and construction. However, when the owner's design expectations do not match reality, or the owner changes something after a decision was made, or the contractor is late in finishing the construction, it often appears that each party has a different understanding of the situation and who should bear responsibility. A written contract serves as a guide that memorializes each party's responsibilities, and how each party agreed to address changes and resolve disputes. Without a written contract there is often a vague recollection of these points, along with a bias towards pushing liability onto others. Time is wasted, money is needlessly spent and bad feelings often remain after disputes are resolved through whatever means become available.

There is no guarantee that a contract will prevent all miscommunications, but there is a much better chance of resolving issues fairly if these basic steps are followed:

1. Use written contracts that coordinate the responsibilities of each party in the project (i.e. owner-architect, owner-contractor);
2. Use AIA Contract Documents because they are the industry standard, are well-coordinated and have time-tested results;
3. Spend adequate time describing project expectations, the scope of services to be provided and each parties' responsibilities;
4. Understand the terms of the contracts and seek legal advice if needed;

5. Use information in the contract (i.e. scope, schedule, budget, change process) as a communication tool in design and construction meetings to ensure that everyone is adhering to the agreed upon terms and that issues are resolved early.

Conclusion

There is no limit to what can go wrong when parties embark on a construction project without a written contract. The horror stories are often based on miscommunications and misaligned expectations about what needs to happen next, how long it will take, and what it will cost. By contrast, a beautiful, well-constructed design that is professionally managed within the parameters of a written contract will have an enduring effect on owners. Using a written contract saves time, money and aggravation.

You and Your Architect

The American Institute of Architects

"Architecture" isn't only for museums, corporations, or the wealthy. Whether you are remodeling the kitchen, creating your dream home, or planning for a future project, working with an architect member of the AIA can save time and money by making your new spaces more functional, comfortable, efficient, and environmentally responsible. Architects play a pivotal role in reducing the overall environmental impact and energy needed to create and operate your home. The result is a project that is beautiful, distinctive, efficient, and healthy for us and the planet. Knowing how to work with your architect will enable you to get the most from this special collaboration.

GETTING STARTED

Whether you have extensive experience with design and construction or are coming to both for the first time, it can be helpful to ask yourself a few questions before interviewing prospective architects.

You do not need firm or complete answers at this point. Rather, these questions will help to ensure that your initial communications will be clear and productive and enable you to select the design professional best suited to your needs.

Questions to ask yourself:

- How will your project be used? Do you have specific ideas on how to translate these activities into spaces and square footage?
- Do you have a site? Or will this also be a subject of discussion with the architect?
- Have you decided upon a schedule and budget?
- What are your overall aspirations for the project—aesthetic and emotional as well as practical?
- Who will be making the critical decisions—you alone, your family, or a committee of some sort?
- Where will the resources come from to create and operate your project?
- Are you willing to pay a little extra up front on systems that will save energy or bring other operations savings and payback over time?
- Will you consider integrating sustainable design strategies in order to reduce negative impacts on the environment, improve the health of occupants, create a more comfortable atmosphere, and improve building performance?
- Do you have previous experience with design and construction? If so, in what ways were you successful, and was the experience in any way disappointing?

A good architect will listen closely to your answers, help you solidify your goals and desires, and translate them into an effective building. Look for a good listener, and you will find a good architect. A list of questions to ask when interviewing prospective architects follows.

Questions to ask the architect

Every architecture firm brings its own combination of skills, expertise, interests, and values to its projects. The challenge is to find the one that aligns most closely with your project's needs. Here are some questions to address when meeting with a prospective architect.

Experience

- What is your design philosophy?
- What sets your firm apart from other architects with similar experience?
- Do you have experience with the building type and size of my project?
- Will you share with me a portfolio of similar projects and provide a list of client references?
- Who from the architecture firm will I be dealing with on a regular basis? Is this the person who will design my project?

My Project

- Are you interested enough in this project to make it a priority?
- What challenges do you foresee for my project?
- What do you see as the important issues or considerations in my project?
- What is your estimated timetable for my project?

- What means will you use to collect information about my needs, goals, etc.?
- How will you help me to fully understand the scope and sequence of the project? Will you utilize models, drawings, or computer animation?

Design

- What are the steps in the design process, and how are they organized?
- What criteria will be used to establish priorities and make design decisions?
- What do you expect me to provide?
- How disruptive will construction be?
- What role do you have during construction?
- Am I expected to work with the contractor directly?

Green Design

- Do you have experience with "green" or sustainable design?
- Do you regularly integrate low or no cost sustainable design strategies into projects?
- Considering the many areas that may be affected by sustainable design, how will you determine which options to pursue?
- If sustainable design technologies are implemented, do up front costs exist that may affect the construction budget? What are the expected pay back times?

Fees

- How do you establish fees?
- In anticipation of a formal proposal with costs, what would you expect your fee to be for this project?
- What is included in your basic services and what services would incur additional fees?
- If the scope of the project changes later in the project, will there be additional fees? How will these fees be justified? How will this be communicated to me?
- What is your track record with completing a project within the original budget?

Selecting Your Architect

Every architecture firm brings its own combination of skills, expertise, interests, and values to its projects. The challenge is to find the one that aligns most closely with your project's needs.

Some of the most frequently asked questions regarding architect selection:

When should I bring the architect into the picture? As early as possible, architects can help you define your project in every respect and may also do site studies, assist in securing planning and zoning approvals, and provide a variety of other predesign services.

Should I meet with more than one firm? Usually, yes. One obvious exception is when you already have a good relationship with an architect.

How do I find suitable firms to contact? Talk to individuals who have developed similar homes and ask who they interviewed. If there are projects that you have admired—whether similar to your own or not—find out who designed them. And your local AIA component will be able to help you identify firms appropriate to your situation and budget and may also maintain referral lists (www.aia.org).

What can I realistically expect to learn from an interview? How can I structure the interview to make it as informative as possible? You can learn how the architect's team will approach your project by talking to key members. Review houses the firm has designed that are similar in type and size to yours or that have addressed similar issues. Find out how the firm will gather information, establish priorities, and make decisions, and what the architect sees as the important issues for consideration. You might also want to inquire about the ability of the architect to stand financially behind the services to be provided. For example, you might ask if the firm carries professional liability insurance, much like that maintained by doctors and lawyers. Indeed, you should choose your architect at least as carefully as you would any other professional provider.

Why are formal interviews desirable? An interview addresses one issue that cannot be covered in brochures: the chemistry between you and the architecture firm.

Should I expect a firm to deliver all the services necessary to complete the project? Not necessarily. You may have considerable project-planning, design, and construction expertise and may be capable of undertaking some tasks yourself. Alternatively, you may find it necessary to add other consultants to the team. Discussion with your architect will establish who will coordinate owner-supplied work or other services.

What is "green" architecture, and do I need to discuss it? "Green" or sustainable design refers to the increasingly popular and important practice of creating architecture that is friendly to both the environment and the end user and the inhabitants. The concepts of sustainable design include:

- Maximization of site potential
- Reduction of non-renewable energy consumption
- Conservation of water
- Reduction of waste
- Use of environmentally friendly products
- Improvement of indoor environmental quality

Using sustainable design strategies may be as simple as using recycled, non-toxic materials or may involve a more comprehensive program incorporating such elements as green roofs, photovoltaic cells that capture sunlight, and air and water treatment systems. Although many firms are generally familiar with green design, you will want to question prospective architects closely about their level of experience in this regard and examine past projects that incorporated sustainable strategies.

How many firms should I interview, and how should they be selected? Typically, three to five firms—enough to see the range of possibilities but not so many that an already tough decision will be further complicated. Treat each firm fairly, offering equal time and access to your site and existing house. Factors such as experience, technical competence, and available staff resources will be important to your decision. Thus, if you are approaching more than one firm, make sure that you can provide all the information required to ensure that the proposals you get offer the same scope of services so that you can evaluate them on a consistent basis.

Project Administration and Management Services	Evaluation and Planning Services	Design Services	Bidding or Negotiation Services	Contract Administration Services	Facility Administration Services
Project administration	Programming	Architectural design documentation	Bidding materials	Submittal services & rejection of defective work	Maintenance & operational programming
Coordination of disciplines/ documents checking	Functional relationships/ flow diagrams	Sustainable design/ documentation	Addenda/responding to bidder inquiries	On-site visits	Start-up assistance
Agency consulting/review approval	Existing facilities surveys	Structural design/ documentation	Bidding/negotiation	Full-time on-site project representative	Record drawing
Value analysis balanced with budget & program	Marketing studies	Mechanical design/ documentation	Analysis of alternates/ substitutions	Testing & inspection administration	Warranty review
Schedule development/ monitoring of the work	Economic feasibility studies	Electrical design/ documentation	Special bidding	Supplemental documentation	Post-contract evaluation
Evaluation of budget & preliminary estimate of cost of the work	Project financing	Civil design/ documentation	Bid evaluation	Quotation requests/ change orders	
Presentation	Site analysis, selection, & development planning	Landscape design/ documentation	Contract award	Contract cost accounting	
Construction management	Detailed site utility studies	Interior design/ documentation		Furniture & equipment installation administration	
	On-site & off-site utility studies	Special design/ documentation		Interpretations & decisions	
	Environmental studies & reports	Material research & specifications		Project close-out	
	Zoning process	Tenant-related service			
	Assistance				

How should I follow up? By soliciting references, ask past clients to assess the performance of both the firm and the resulting architecture. Notify the selected firm or short-listed firms as soon as possible to ensure their availability.

On what should I base my decision? Personal confidence in the architect is paramount. Seek also an appropriate balance among design ability, technical competence, professional service, and cost.

Selection Is a Mutual Process

The most thoughtful architects are as careful in selecting their clients as owners are in selecting architects. Be prepared to answer questions about your project's purpose, budget, time frame, site, and the team of players you anticipate being involved with the project.

And don't be afraid to be frank. Tell the architect what you know and what you expect. Ask for an explanation of anything you do not understand. The more you put on the table at the outset, the better the chances are for a successful project. As client and architect jointly evaluate alternative approaches to the project's direction, priorities are clarified, and new possibilities emerge. There is no substitute for the intensive dialogue and inquiry that characterize the design process.

Services Available from Architects

As the owner, you will find it helpful to review this chart with your architect to acquaint yourself with the professional services your project may require. Ask your architect for an explanation of any unfamiliar terms or processes.

Negotiating the Agreement

The formal agreement between you and your architect is an opportunity to ensure that you both envision the same project, requirements, and expectations. Before committing these to paper, use the steps presented below to identify any items that may have been missed.

Establish project requirements with these crucial questions:

- What is to be designed and built?
- Where will (or might) it be built?
- What is the level of quality?
- What is the role of the project in your life, your community, and/or your business?
- What are the scheduling requirements or restraints?
- What is the target date for completion?
- What are the budget and sources of financing?
- Who are the anticipated key team members?

Describe project tasks and assign responsibility for each one

You and your architect should clarify the administrative, design, and construction tasks essential to successfully completing the project, as well as the services required and who will be responsible for each of them.

Identify your schedule requirements.

Place all tasks on a time line, estimating duration for each, and identify those that, if delayed, will postpone completion of your project. Compare the time line with your target completion date and adjust one or both as appropriate.

Take a critical look at the results.

Good project schedules allow enough time for decision making. Is your schedule reasonable, particularly given the project's requirements and budget? Have you allowed enough time to review the architect's submissions, receive any necessary approvals, and make your decisions?

Compensating Your Architect

The fee an architect receives depends on the types and levels of services provided, and the formal agreement you develop jointly with your architect will be an excellent basis for a compensation proposal. There are a number of commonly used payment structures— compensation may be based on one or more of them—and arriving at the one that is fairest to both client and architect requires thoughtful consideration.

- Multiple of Direct Personnel Expense multiplies salaries plus benefits by a factor representing overhead and profit.
- Professional Fee Plus Expenses includes salaries, benefits, and overhead as the expense, and the fee may be a multiplier, percentage, or lump sum.
- Hourly Billing Rates include salaries, benefits, overhead, and profit in rates for designated personnel.
- Stipulated Sum. Compensation is stated as a dollar amount.
- Percentage of Cost of the Work. Compensation is calculated by applying an agreed-upon percentage to the estimated or actual cost of the work.
- Square Footage. Compensation equals the square footage of the structure multiplied by a pricing factor.
- Unit Cost. Compensation is based on the number of units such as rooms.

The Custom Residential Architects Network

The Custom Residential Architects Network (CRAN) Knowledge Community develops knowledge and information about custom residential practice. CRAN presents information and facilitates the exchange of knowledge and expertise to promote the value of design.

Publishers' note: Alessina Brooks and Paul Latham would like to thank Dr. Richard Hayes and the Custom Residential Architects Network (CRAN) for their efforts in producing this superb collection of houses.

Selection Committee

David S.R. Andreozzi, NCARB, AIA
Andreozzi Architects

Mark Demerly, AIA, LEED AP
Demerly Architects

Luis Jauregui, AIA
Jauregui Architecture, Interior Designs & Construction

Jean Rehkamp Larson, AIA
Rehkamp Larson Architects Inc.

Andrew Porth, AIA, LEED AP
Porth Architects

AIA National Component Staff Support

Richard L. Hayes PhD, AIA Editor-in-Chief

Bruce Bland, CRAN Liaison

Virginia Ebbert, Manager, Architect's Knowledge Resource

Nancy Hadley, Assoc. AIA, CA, DAS, Project Curator

Ann Harris, Project Assistance

Susan Parish, CRAN Liaison

Photography Credits

Aaron Thomas Killen 206–211

Accent Photography 130–135

Alise O'Brien 66–71

Amir Sultan and the Architect 174–179

Anice Hoachlander 44–47

Benjamin Benschneider 14–19, 106–111, 112–117

Bill Timmerman Photography 216–221

Brian Vanden Brink 82–87, 100–105

Bruce Damonte 94–99

Courtesy of the Architect (NAGA) 200–205

Derek Skalko and Altitude Filmworks 20–23

Erik Laignel and Jacob Sadrak 88–93

Ethan Kaplan and Joe Fletcher 72–77

Evan Thomas 78–81

Frank Oudeman 154–159

Ian Macdonald-Smith and Ann Spurling 162–167

Jeff Goldberg and Halkin Mason Photography 148–153

John McManus Photographer 168–173

Jud Haggard Photography 136–141

Juergen Nogai 60–65

Ken McCown and Robert Batey 124–129

Nic LeHoux 26–31

Paul Crosby 32–37

Paul Stevenson Oles, FAIA 194–199

Peter Aaron/OTTO 180–185

Richard Mandelkorn 142–147

Steve Keating Photography 48–53

Susan Gilmore and the Architect 10–13

Timothy Hursley, Mark Howell, and Roy T. Decker 186–191

Tony Soluri Photography 54–59

Warren Jagger 38–43, 118–123

Wayne Lloyd, AIA and Kate Russell Photography 212–215

Index of Architects

The planet exhibits many climate zones depending on how fine a gradation one would like to make. The four used within this book were chosen to allow for solutions applicable to a range of similar conditions.